art by: Chris Szostek 1

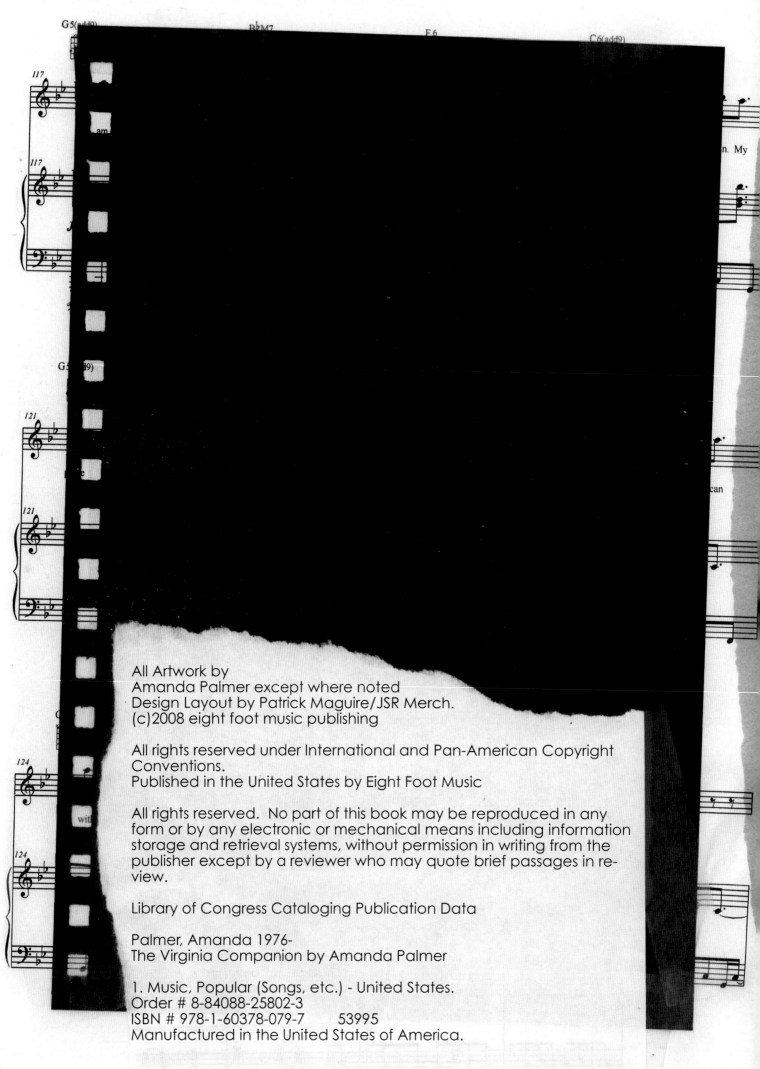

All Artwork by
Amanda Palmer except where noted
Design Layout by Patrick Maguire/JSR Merch.
(c)2008 eight foot music publishing

Library of Congress Cataloging Publication Data

Palmer, Amanda 1976-
The Virginia Companion by Amanda Palmer

1. Music, Popular (Songs, etc.) - United States.
Order # 8-84088-25802-3
ISBN # 978-1-60378-079-7   53995
Manufactured in the United States of America.

THE DRESDEN DOLLS

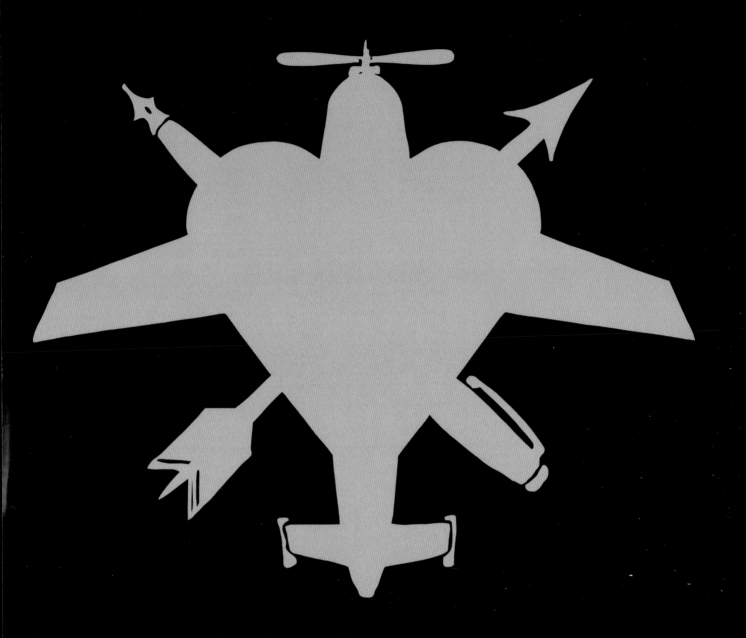

The Virginia Companion

Amanda Palmer

Brian Viglione

photo by: Kenneth Thomas

TABLE of CONTENTS

for the

PIANOFORTE

SECOND SERIES

Arranged, Adapted

Never Enough Thanks — 9
Dear Comrade — 18
The Recordings — 62
Allaire — 64
Camp Street — 88
Mad Oak — 92
The Artworks — 102
The Art of Barnaby Whitfield — 114
The Fan Art — 124
Notes for the Player — 135

Sheet Music – Yes, Virginia...

1. Sex Changes — 151
2. Backstabber — 165
3. Modern Moonlight — 175
4. My Alcoholic Friends — 186
5. Delilah — 194
6. Dirty Business — 207
7. First Orgasm — 218
8. Mrs. O. — 224
9. Shores of California — 232
10. Necessary Evil — 242
11. Mandy Goes to Med School — 252
12. Me and the Mini-Bar — 266
13. Sing — 274

"There is No Virginia"

1. Dear Jenny — 283
2. Night Reconnaisance — 295
3. The Mouse and the Model — 305
4. Ultima Esperanza — 314
5. The Gardener — 325
6. Lonesome Organist Rapes Page Turner — 334
7. Sorry Bunch — 344
8. The Kill — 350
9. The Sheep Song — 358
10. Boston — 364
The Dresden Dolls on Tour 2004-2006 — 377

THE

BOSTON: 1

7

Ponies by: Amanda Palmer

ACKNOWLEGEDMENTS

Yes, Virginia....Many Kind People Helped Us With This Book.

The Band would like to thank...

Emily "Wizzle" White. The Best Ever.
Laura "Miss Merch" Keating. Queen of Wares and other Knowledges.
Katie Kay. Rocks Every Hat with Style. Vagina Power!
Sydney Wayser. Lydia Berg-Hammond. = Ninja Interns.
Mike Luba. Suck It.
Madison House. Home of Making Things Go.
David Bason & Roadrunner. For believing in us.
Kevin Morris. Welcome to the Family.
Jenny Applebaum. For coming along, too. You're killing it.
Mark Berger. For Endless Patience and Beautiful Art.
Wes Bockley, Mandy & all of JSR. Helping us with all things Tangible.
Sheri Hausey & Bill T. Milller. For Going the Extra Media Mile.
Patrick, Elaine and Phil at PS Business Mgmt. For keeping us Not Broke.
Bill H, Sean and Rick @ BRAT. For making Us Go on the Net.
Matt Hickey & High Road. For booking our asses with extreme style.
Neil Warnock, Jesse Hunter & The Agency Group. Same, but extreme European Style.
Matthew Kaplan. For Having the Best 45 Vinyl Collection of Any Lawyer.
Lee Barron. For Creating the most wonderful Place To Be From.
Max Melton. Our favorite Pretentious Cunt. Thank You for Exisiting (and doing some Errands).
Becca Rosenthal. For helping out while Wearing Shades at most times.
Amandacera Hannon. Gorgeous Hand on Deck In Boston.
All of our Folks and Friends. For Being There.

These folks were the life blood and building blocks of this project. Without them, nothing:

Anabel Vázquez. For keeping the Mountain of Photos under control.
Patrick Maguire. For Kicking even More Ass The 2nd Time Around. Here's to the Perfect Mess.
Howie Kenty. For creating Notation where there would be None. You're a prince.

We would like to thank, with as deep and wide a Thank as we can muster in print, all the photographers and artists who took so much time and energy out of their lives to help us create this. Usually without getting paid, always for the love of Rock Love: you are the Art Party. Thank you, thank you, thank you.

We would like to thank all of our fans. You know who you are, and you know what you're doing. Whatever you're doing, KEEP DOING IT, because IT'S WORKING!!! IT'S WORKING!!!!!!!!!!!!

See you out there.
Amanda would especially like to thank.....

...the awesome folkses who helped me edit the text for this book,
thank them deeply for their insights, patience and grammar fascism:

Bill H. For helping with editing...above and beyond, as usual.
Geeta Dayal. For jumping is last minute with your Bad-Ass Skillz.
Beth Hommel. Your feedback has been beyond wonderful. I am lucky to know you.
and as always:
Anthony Martignetti. For Always Calling me on my Shit.

...and I would also like to thank my comrade, Brian Viglione. Thank you for working with me
on this book, thank you for drumming like nobody else, thank you for looking hot in a dress
and thank you for staying in this adventure despite its hardships.
Our connection is my greatest teacher.
Through thick and thin, O My Brother. I love you.

photo by: Sheri Hausey

photo by: Tina Korhonen

photo by: Lauren Goldberg/fairytalevegas.com

photo by: Todd Owyoung

photo by: Sara Travis

photos by: Taylor Crothers

Dear Comrade,

Welcome to the second installment. I hope you enjoy it. Sorry it took so long...again. This book is being released a full two years after the release of Yes, Virginia..., its companion album. Most artists release their sheet-music books and corresponding albums simultaneously. I guess I don't.

I just read the intro to the last book (The Dresden Dolls Companion, which also came out over two years after our first record) to see what it might inspire. I found this:

"...I cannot imagine going through this process a second time with the sheet music for the new record..." (p. 3)

A-fucking-men. As with the last one, I had a hard time sitting down to write the text for this book. I finally realized where this procrastination stems from. It's out of a kind of respect on the part of my designer-book-putter-together-self to my actual song-writer-music-maker self. Putting out this book as the same time as the record would have been like fucking a new person the day you get divorced. No, that's wrong. It would've been like insisting you're going to be sober for life when you still have a hangover. That's closer. It's like... hanging your painting on the wall while the paint is still wet.

No, wait, got it: It's like going to the theater to watch a movie and staying in your seat at the end to watch the behind-the-scenes documentary about the making of the movie. It's a downer, man. It spoils the magic.

Tearing apart and exposing the artistic process while you're inside of it is not only unhealthy for the art in question; it's unhealthy for the artist. The hall of internal mirrors becomes smudged by the sticky fingers of the inner child, with smears of annoying finger paint clouding the filter of perception. The transmuting internalized self implodes as the psyche shuts down to protect itself from being exposed to its own methodology.

Gotcha. I'm actually just a lazy fuck.

If you're not familiar with the first book, may I suggest you run out and purchase a copy for more in-depth enlightenment regarding my creative process. In this new book, I shall not further bore you with details of my creative neurosis, procrastinations and second-guesses regarding the songwriting and book-making process.*

Instead—for I do wish, as always, to further enlighten you about my state of mental affairs--I have instead edited down a voluminous series of late-night haikus exchanged by Sean Slade (a.k.a. Stutz, a.k.a. Ikiru, a.k.a. the producer of Yes, Virginia... and No, Virginia...) and myself, spanning the time period July 2005 - April, 2006.

*If you are keen to join the freak-fest and are too poor to buy a copy of the first book, many insights into all of these shortcomings may also be found on my blog:www.dresdendolls.com/diary or www.myspace.com/whokilledamandapalmer

-----Original Message-----

om: Amanda Palmer
nt: Saturday, July 02, 2005 6:32 PM
: Sean Slade
bject: My haiku for the night

ter the sun sets
n duran duran tonight
m new woman

n Jul 9, 2005, at 8:03 PM, Sean Slade
ote:

y haiku for the night:

y sweet darling, your
aikus are you completely
ore more more more more

kay , the last line might be cheating,
 t it's very glam rock, kinda like the
nd who invoked your apostasy.)

iru

om: Amanda Palmer
bject: d2
ate: July 10, 2005 1:58:35 AM EDT
: Sean Slade

simon LeBon
hy the dream is distorted
d too old to fuck

om: Sean Slade
nt: Saturday, July 09, 2005 11:49 PM
bject: Haiku

utright perfidy!
asputin would not submit
his dethronement!

iru

om: Amanda Palmer
ate: July 10, 2005 11:30:35 PM EDT
: Sean Slade

aches out for love
e-night stands are so shameful
hen the sex ain't good

om: Amanda Palmer
bject: Re: Today's Haiku
ate: July 22, 2005 12:25:13 AM
: Sean Slade

hy go to yoga
espite rock hard abs and ass
ill surely die

From: Amanda Palmer
Date: August 9, 2005 5:24:37 AM EDT
To: Sean Slade

wake at four-thirty
sit on roof to meditate
sparrows and sirens

the heart turns frigid
leftover indian food
is my only choice

On Aug 9, 2005, at 4:13 AM, Sean
Slade wrote:

Jet Lag up the Butt
Computers cease to Function;
Nietzsche Cheeseburger.

Tokyo Hotel Room.
I can't let the Japanese
Waiter see me cry.

-Ikiru

From: Amanda Palmer
Subject: Late night Haiku
Date: August 10, 2005 7:25:09 AM EDT
To: Sean Slade

simple is simple
good day and bad piano
avoid the drama

On Aug 10, 2005, at 5:27 AM, Sean
Slade wrote:

Sweet Sweet Anarchy
Whatever Happens Happens
Embrace The Chaos

Ikiru

On Aug 11, 2005, at 4:15 AM, Sean
Slade wrote:

Fleetwood Recording.
Listened to Mrs. O six
Times in a Row. Done.

-Producer Dude

On Aug 11, 2005, at 7:21 PM, Sean
Slade wrote:

Tree limb with sleeping
Squirrel. Was he asleep or dead?
I wondered. He woke.

Ikiru

(I wrote this while I was on the
Phone with you this morning.
Please forgive my presumption
that the rodent was male.)

From: Amanda Palmer
Subject: Window Haiku
Date: August 12, 2005 11:54:23 AM EDT
To: Sean Slade

hmmmm.

riding bicycle
pigeon corpse lies in puddle
bad drinking water

On Mar 13, 2006, at 10:24 AM, Sean
Slade wrote:

Are you in slumber
or sweet, sentient, and alive,
at least in theory.

-Stutz

From: Amanda Palmer
Date: March 13, 2006 4:39:57 PM EST
To: Sean Slade

i am in a deep
paradoxical and sweet
hangover skankdom

From: Sean Slade
Subject: Re: Haiku
Date: March Mar 15, 2006 4:19 PM EST
To: Amanda Palmer

My new favorite book:
the dictionary, filled with
words to be employed.

-Stutz

From: Amanda Palmer
Subject: Re: Haiku
Date: March 16, 2006 5:00:48 AM
To: Sean Slade

my new favorite book:
the phone book, with so many
souls i'll never harm

On Apr 15, 2006, at 12:19 AM, Sean
Slade wrote:

In contemplation
Methinks the Sky God laughs much
More than Satan does.

-Stutz

On Apr 15, 2006, at 12:41 AM,
Amanda Palmer wrote:

we're all gonna die
he who survives to laugh last
laughs the loneliest

From: Sean Slade
Date: April 15, 2006 12:57:10 AM EDT
To: Amanda Palmer

For the human face,
Cackles, wild laughter and tears
are equivalent.

-Stutz

art by: Rebecca McMaster
based on a photo by:
Robert E. Klein

How MUCH DID YOU ARCHIVE
& how much did you feel
and how much did you waste
trying to prove that
                    it was real

            (you were real)

        (you were here)

photo by: Lauren Goldberg/fairytalevegas.com

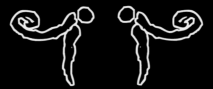

photo by: Diana Yanez – www.dianayanez.com

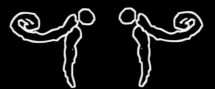

I LOVE YOU...

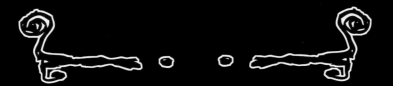

Photo by Doriano Zunino, Styling by Alex Vaccani, Project Coordinator: Marco Cresci

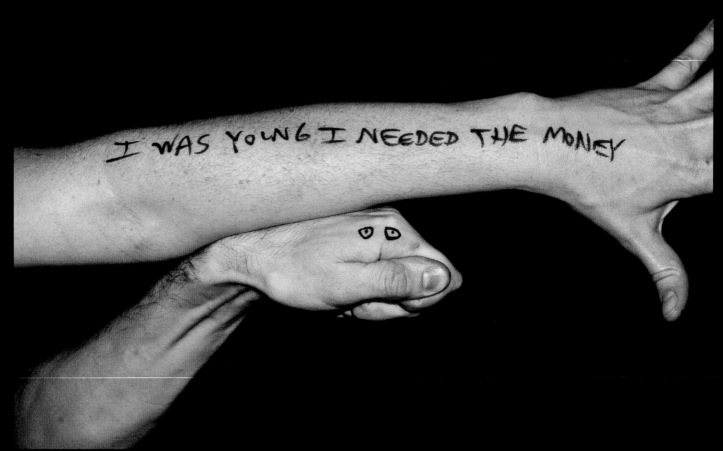

photo by: Lauren Goldberg/fairytalevegas.com

photo by: Gregory Nomoora

art by: Blake Starr

Yes, Virginia ////////////

I exercise my personal freedom
when I order two beers and bum
a cigarette and smoke it. I spend all
day dreading and regretting this
very moment.
I almost feel free. Unencumbered.

photo by: Pierre Veillet aka TRIP FONTAINE

art by: Lindsey Kahn

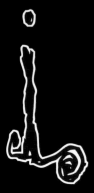

photo by: Todd Owyoung

33

photo by: Taylor Crothers

photo by: Todd Owyoung

photo by: Todd Owyoung

art by: Danielle Charron

photo by Peter Dean

photo by: Ron Nordin

photo by: Kelly Davidson

photo by: Susan San Giovanni

photo by: Martyn Wheatley, sinisterpictures.co.uk

photo by: Lauren Goldberg/fairytalevegas.com

decide. Just do. I barely think
of myself as a musician. I'm
not, really. It's an accident.
I'm not interested in music the
way other people are. It moves
me, but it moves everybody.
I don't obsess. I don't get excited.
It's not the passion of my life.
Mix it with theater and it
get closer. But

Yes, Virginia...

There is no Virginia

photo by: Amanda Palmer

art by: Barnaby Whitfield

57

@ = I like these lyrics and they told my soul.

Mrs. O @
backrubber
sex changes
~~~~~ mm
BBQ
first O. @
stones ●
Boston ~~~ minibar @
~~~~~~~~~~~~~~~~~~
(10)

def.

glass slip @
the kill A
sing ★
lonesome
listerine   maybe
gardener
dirty bizness ★
awful detail
horse + model
alcoholic friends @
mary @
ultima

amsterdam
pierre   lovers

airplanes
whiting girl   ?
follow
→ mary's surgeon
provanity
christopher lyons
→ flinty whacks
→ have to drive
love is still possible

~~~~ minibar
→ Koledina - -
→ R+K - -   Solo
another year another year
hey bitch - .
5 + ambien - .

BLAKE SAYS?
strength thru music

LA →   manner of speaking
THUR   the gypsy — |DD|

          minibar
          Koledina
          Rhyme + Rythm
          another year
          hey bitch
          ambien
          blake says
          strength thru music
          gypsy
          linden tree

          matter of speaking
          holocaust
          cosmic dancer
→   mamas lied

wrong maybe

BILL OF THE PLAY

FOUNDED 1908 **5TH SEASON**

GAIETY THEATRE

The Dresden Dolls PRESENT Yes, Virginia...

CAST OF CHARACTERS

Vocals, Piano, Mellotron & Organ ....Amanda Palmer
Drums, Percussion, Vocals, Bass & Guitar ....Brian Viglione
Produced by ....Sean Slade, Paul Q. Kolderie & The Dresden Dolls
Mixed by ....Paul Q. Kolderie
Engineered by ....Paul Q. Kolderie & Adam Taylor
Sing Choir...Holly Brewer & M@ McNiss
Delilahs..Holly Brewer, Whitney Moses & Mali Sastri

Recorded at Allaire Studios, Shokan, NY and Camp Street Studios, Cambridge, MA. Assistant Engineer at Allaire: Matt Snedecor.
Mastered at Sterling Sound, NYC by George Marino.
All songs written by Amanda Palmer & published by Eight Foot Music (ASCAP)
A & R: David Bason. Front cover drawing by Amanda Palmer
Artwork, design & layout by Amanda Palmer and Sarah Gensert & Mark Berger, Madison House Design. Creative Director: Jeff Chenault
Photographs of abandoned theatre spaces by Nicholas Vargelis. Black and white photo of The Dresden Dolls by Scott Irivine
Booklet back cover: E. Stephen Frederick, with thanks to the Empire S.N.A.F.U. Archives
Propaganda posters by Barnaby Whitfield. Booklet back cover: Zea Barker
Theater artists: *Sex Changes:* Nura Tafeche; *Backstabber:* Gécédille; *Modern Moonlight:* Alec Johnson, S. Adrienne Elder, Chelsea Shannon; *Delilah:* Sheena Antoinette Seago, Die Booth, Emy Koopman, Leila Marlene von Meyer; *Dirty Business:* Barnaby Whitfield; *First Orgasm:* Tracy Christenson; *Mrs. O.:* Dustin Parker; *Shores of California:* Zoe B. Kraus; *Necessary Evil/Mandy Goes to Med School:* Blake Gentry, Avalon Batory, Holly Hutchings, Claudia Drake, Joseph Kranz; *Me & the Minibar/Sing:* Jessica Kincl
Far more artwork, photos & other unsavory items inspired by The Dresden Dolls and *Yes, Virginia* can be found at www.dresdendolls.com.
Our deepest gratitude goes out to every single person who submitted art for this project.
Management: Mike Luba for Madison House Inc. - www.madisonhouseinc.com

A standing ovation for those without whom we'd be nothing: mike luba, bart dahl & madison house, lee barron & the cloud club foundation, emily white & the white family, david bason & roadrunner records, joel siminches, michael pope, zea barker, noah blumenson-cook, the martin bros., bill h, jon whitney @ brainwashed.com, ma, pa & maia viglione, mutti & johann, jack, donna & alex palmer, anthony & laura, ron nordin, brendon downey, robert fulop, whitney moses, casey porter, edward ka-spel & the legendary pink dots, clara lafrance, desi & mark, murray barg, bri olson, walter mcdonough, dave macnamara, mark kates @ fenway, andrew anselmo, david franklin, oedipus, harvey leeds, lesley dean, stan & judy viglione, dave mcglocklin & johnny parretti, josh & alina, matt hickey, josh boyle, becca rosenthal, anna vogelzang, mark baxter, deborah adams, krin haglund, jonas woolverton, jessica fox, cormac bride, andrew kopacz, greg michalowski and jack's drum shop, vic firth drumsticks and zildjian cymbals.

"Ah, Virginia, in all this world there is nothing else real and abiding..." - Francis P. Church, *The New York Sun,* 1897

March 24, 2005
Nashoba Brook Bakery
10:30 am

Another school shooting, another flood of
tears over green tea at the checkered
table. The children are killing the children.
Don't be afraid. Don't stop your
drawing. Don't judge. The children.

Sean is coming over in an hour and
a half and we'll be making decisions
about album tracks. I don't know
what I want anymore. All the songs
are blurring together into a haze.
Sing for the children starting the children.

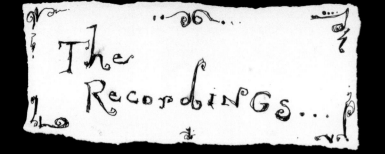

ABOUT THE RECORDING

I first met Sean Slade when he came to observe us playing at the Middle East as part of the local battle of the bands. I found him through a mutual friend and mailed him our first CD with a letter and a plea. The Great Sean Slade and Paul Q. Kolderie (Sean's long-time engineering partner) had worked with Radiohead, the Pixies, Dinosaur Jr. and a long laundry list of amazing bands at the legendary Fort Apache Studios in the 1990s. The studio had since been re-named Camp St. for weird legal reasons I never figured out.

I remember that first conversation downstairs at the Middle East; Sean invited us to come record a free song at Camp St. so we could get to know each other (which we did – that's where "The Mouse and the Model" came from—see song notes).

So when the time came to pick a producer for Yes, Virginia, we picked Sean and Paul and started on lists and pre-production around March of 2005. We were touring here and there, but we would meet with Sean at our rehearsal space, play him songs, give him demos, meet in restaurants. He and I would chat and chat and exchange email haikus.

Sean was going through a divorce at the time and things were heavy. The band was about to go to Japan for a quick promotional trip (and to play Fuji Rock, a huge festival there) and Sean, being the spontaneous rock and roll type that he is, decided to join us. The trip really bonded us together. We were going through our own hard times that summer; Brian and I were both exhausted from touring and the relentless schedule (in retrospect, careening straight into the second album without taking a break was a terrible, terrible idea) and life took on a super-surreal quality for a while.

We came home and in August of 2005 we recorded all of the demos (19 total) at Fleetwood Studios, a strange old 1960s ramshackle studio in Revere, Massachusetts. The recordings really aren't very good—we went back and examined then to see if any of them were worth releasing on No, Virginia, but we just weren't in top form. The sounds were weird since the studio was random and my voice was in shit shape. Out of that pile of songs, "Awful Detail," "Have to Drive," "Ultima Esperanza" and "Glass Slipper" all hit the cutting room floor and were axed from the possibility of getting onto the record. "The Kill," "Boston," "Lonesome Organist" and "Gardener" would all be recorded at Allaire but were ultimately left off as well.

Allaire Studios was chosen by Sean and Paul; it was a rustic mansion atop a huge mountain in upstate New York that had recently been converted to a state-of-the-art live-in studio. It was extremely remote. To drive to the bottom of the mountain took fifteen minutes and from there, the nearest gas station was still several miles. Woodstock was the nearest town, about a 30-minute drive away.

The place itself was huge and beautiful. There was a majestic view out of every window, wonderful food cooked by a full-time staff, 247 kinds of amps and guitars, a big green lawn, a pool, and a path leading up to a lookout tower at the tip-top of the mountain. If you looked to the left from the tower, you could see David Bowie's mountain. Apparently he went to Allaire and liked it so much he decided to buy the next mountain over. We would commence work at around 1 or 2 pm every day and work until about 10 or 11. This process was about as different as you could get from the process of our first album, which was made in Martin Bisi's giant cave in Brooklyn, with city life right outside the door. Everyone loved it but me. I freaked out and got cabin fever within five minutes of arrival. Brian was in heaven. I think my journal entries from that week or two will tell a better story than I can. After 10 full days, we left Allaire with the basics for 17 songs on half-inch tape.

Sept 10th, 2005 • Woodstock Center on the Grass, NY • 2 pm • Saturday

Arrived. With no expectation about anything and very little thought given to what the quality of time here would taste like. I was thrown into a minor sad panic last night. I still don't know completely why. Upon arrival at Allaire I felt the isolated choking grip and being isolated up here alone...away from my lifeblood...I didn't want the woods, or a view, or a pool, or people serving me food. This seems to have nothing to do with the songs I wrote that I now need to record with my band. Why on earth are we here?...
It all feels wrong and lonely and strange. I woke up this morning with a heavy heart until it hit me. It was like an instant replay from the moment in Butterfield at Wesleyan my freshman year when I realized I was NOT TRAPPED...I had a car and could drive back to Boston and back to Cafe Pamplona. To read. If I wanted to. It might be a two-hour drive, but Fuck It. So I realized this morning that I don't HAVE to stay sequestered up in the lap of studio luxury even though Sean assumed we would all never leave. Woodstock is a half-hour drive, and it's beautiful here and perfect. I went to a yoga class and found a cafe with internet and am sitting on the grass in the middle of town watching the hippie kids who look like a rural version of the pit punks from Harvard Square...A woman near me is holding up a tie-dyed sheet that reads "families for peace" and she's flashing the peace sign at all the bypassing cars who are waving back. A man across the street was sitting on a wall playing "tangled up in blue". Now a man on a bench near me, with a different guitar is playing a serene acoustic version of "I wanna be sedated"...there are dogs everywhere...it's time, I should go. But I don't want to. I don't want to go to Allaire and face conflict. On tour there is the constant diversion of motion. Now there is a girl with blue and blond and black hair sitting near me with a pad of paper, drawing. I can see my next ten days mapped out much more nicely that I have this escape, a yoga studio, and a plan to Be Away. I don't care how delicious the food up there is, down here I feel free. There are banjos and cigarettes and yelling and dogs. I like it here better. Banjo-man and Ramones guy are collaborating. They're playing "you are my sunshine" in a minor key.

Sept 13, 2005 • Woodstock Center, NY • Bread Alone • 11:27 am • Monday

Things have gotten better but there's still a sinking feeling...no matter...we'll get good takes and put this thing together one way or another. The songs. The songs. We've plowed through "Backstabber" (no good takes), "Shores" (no good takes), "Mrs. O" (maybe one good take), "Alcoholic Friends" (one, we think), "Dirty Business" (none that really worked), "Boston (one ok take) and "First Orgasm" at the tail end of the night where I let my voice go into the Marianne Faithfull pit of hell where it was leading me. It's interesting how I can fight the fry but I often just let it rip just to let the producers and engineers know not to push me. My voice woke up feeling swollen and haggard from all the singing. Yesterday was spent driving to Lew Beach for Auntie Anne's funeral.... just peace in my heart watching people lower one of their own into the ground. Over and over this happens. Allaire is strange and beautiful but feels like the Overlook Hotel from The Shining. I come here to Woodstock Center to feed, needing human life like a junkie fix. Just to see and hear. I don't need to interact. When I was little on divorce weekends at Jack's in NYC, the city noise coming from the window would lull me to sleep in minutes whereas I would spend fitful hours awake in the dark at home in Lexington in the deafening silence of the wooded suburbs. I needed and loved to feel the earth moving and the cars crashing and the yelling and flow of human traffic. All was well. In the silence I just heard loneliness. Sirens are beautiful. They remind me that there are some compassionate parts of civilization. After this day, six to go. I'm not worried about the recording. It's going to be fine. Sean and Paul are magic.

Sept 15, 2005 • Woodstock Center, NYC • Bread Alone • 11:27 am • Wednesday

...Yesterday's tracking went well. We got a good "Sing," a good "Sex Changes," a good "Kill," a good "Necessary." We have a good "Modern Moonlight" and a good "Boston"....we need a "Shores," a "Backstabber," an "Orgasm," a "Minibar" and another "Mandy" and "Mrs. O." So many songs. It's going well and I feel fully out the woods adjustment-wise.

Sept 16, 2005 • Some Yoga Teacher's Driveway • Woodstock NY • 9:42 am • Friday

...Today Em and Luba and Bason and Bart are making the trek up to see the studio. Tracking yesterday was amazing. We got four takes in one afternoon—
"Shores," "Backstabber," "Mrs. O" and "Mandy" all within a few hours. I'm feeling better about everything. We have three more days here plus one morning and we'll spend them mostly on overdubs and fixes. Brian is out of his depression as well and bouncing around in his kilt like a nymph.

Sept 25, 2005 • Boston • Noon

We begin vocals today. I am ready.

Oct 5, 2005 • Boston • Nashoba Cafe • 1:30

Fuck me.

Life is moving at an uncomfortable pace and I'm spending days mixing at Camp Street, mornings knocking things over and nights trying to get the fucking Dresden Dolls Companion ready to ship to the layout designer. What can I say. I'm ashamed of myself as a singer, a songwriter and a piano player. Wasn't I supposed to be better than this?

The record is sounding like....I don't know what....proof mostly.

Oct 10th 2005 • Cambridge • Cafe Pamplona • 1 pm

Ah, the pre-tour frenzy. Tonight will be manic packing and last minute what-the-fuck with the sheet music book.

Aaaaaaaaaaaaaaaaaaaaaaaaaaaaaaaaaaaaaaaaaaaaaah.

The Recording is almost finished. It's been unreal and too easy. I don't know what to make of it, honestly. So I stopped trying.

I want to live here.

Things feel settled, under control and it's coming from inside this time. I feel less shakable. I'm in it. I'm here.

We put on finishing touches and mixed the entire record back at home in Boston at Camp St. While we were there, we also recorded the cover of "Pretty in Pink" (which is included on No, Virginia) and an extra few B-sides for the record (one of Neutral Milk Hotel's "Two-Headed Boy," which went onto to the Japanese import, and one of Jane's Addiction's "I Would For You," with Brian on bass). Mixing went by quickly and without drama. In fact, I barely remember it, but there are pictures, so I must have been there. Reading back in my journal, I was doing four other Things, no wonder. It was around then that I thought it might be fun to dress everybody up in Revolutionary War-Era costumes. Sean wanted to be Ben Franklin, Paul wanted to be Thomas Jefferson and Adam wanted to be Aaron Burr (the third vice-president of the United States also famous for mortally wounding Alexander Hamilton). We mastered the whole beast in NYC at Sterling Sound with George Marino, and the record was Done.

Recording the extra songs for No, Virginia was an entirely different affair. We booked a local Boston studio called Mad Oak, went in and banged out the tracks, vocals and mix in under five days. We found the evil stuffed Santa under one of the old pianos. It was Fate, obviously. I took him all around the studio for an exciting photo shoot while Sean and Benny (the engineer) worked on the EQ.

No, Virginia was also mastered down in NYC with George Marino. It was the first mastering session I'd never attended; Brian went down but I was in Seattle with Jason Webley producing the debut album by the wonderfully talented conjoined twin sisters Evelyn and Evelyn Nevel.

And there you have it.

Allaire
catskill Mtns, New york

Allaire Studios, at the time I was there redeemed my faith that life, at times, could be merciful. The fact that we had been presented with the opportunity to record our second album there felt like some kind of divine intervention. The atmosphere of the entire experience helped to counteract all of the fear and anxiety that I felt leading up to the recording. This studio, which stood overlooking the Ashokan Reservoir and the surrounding valleys, was a place I could feel recharged and focused on giving the best performances possible. The seclusion in the beautiful wilderness was a welcome change for me from all of the airports, busses, and overall cluster-fuck that I was used to from touring for two solid years. There were none of the distractions of everyday city life. No traffic, pushing crowds, noise, or advertisements, polluting the landscape. It seemed to offer all the things that would keep my energy up and not feel bored or trapped when I was done with my work; I could sleep soundly, I could eat well, and I could crank a gold-sparkle Les Paul through a Marshall full-stack up in my bedroom and play thrash metal at 10:16 am and not get in trouble. It was paradise.

From a musician-geek/ technical standpoint, Allaire had every tool of the trade, trick in the book, and last detail covered, to use at your disposal short of Keith Richards smoking a joint in the corner. It was miraculous. It was also reassuring to watch Paul Colderie and Sean Slade salivating all over the gear that they had at their fingertips. There were microphone inputs everywhere; the hallways, the bathroom, 80ft. up in the rafters of The Great Hall, which was a gorgeous, all wood room, roughly the shape of a small cathedral. The drums were recorded in there with the intent to take advantage of the incredible natural reverb that to me, sounded like I was playing atop Mt. Olympus. Getting our gear situated in the tracking rooms was one thing, however fitting the two 88 key Kurtzweil keyboards, a five piece drum kit, seats, stands, cymbal bags, cables, a box of 42 drum heads, three suitcases, several bags of food, several Space Pillows, and We Two Dolls into one, very beleaguered, but valiant Volvo station wagon was another matter altogether. It felt like I drove all the way from Boston to Shokan, NY with my knees on the dash and my forehead pressed against the windshield. Then, climbing the mile long road that zigzagged its way up the mountainside to the studio gates made you feel like you were on some kind of safari expedition. Man, talk about building the suspense—just when you think you may pitch off the side of a cliff, you arrive at the entrance gate.

My daily routine there was simple and satisfying: Wake, Eat, Stretch, Rock. In my downtime, I would take various combinations of guitars and amps to my room to work on parts, or go play outside. Some memories that stand out are one time were actually running

photo by: Amanda Palmer

outside while a reel of tape was being changed out and going for a swim in the pool outside, then dashing back in to do another take. Also walking around the woods, exploring the rest of the house, which was sort of eerily off-limits, like the house of the mysterious uncle in The Secret Garden. Not once did I feel the need to leave the mountain for the entire eleven days that we were there. I loved the quiet calm of the warm, early-autumn days, breathing the clean air days, the joy of getting to play drums in a beautiful place everyday. I wanted to remain immersed in it. It felt sacred and ceremonial. I decided to wear only a kilt that Amanda had given me for every song I tracked. Seems funny to me now, but at the time, I had promised myself to push harder than I ever had before, because to be honest, Yes, Virginia was almost never made. I actually had to be talked into recording it.

The three and a half years leading up to September of 2005 were the most horrifyingly complicated and demanding times I have ever experienced. The excitement of watching our band take flight and seeing my dreams manifest before my eyes was often marred by an extremely painful navigation of interpersonal conflict, a complex working relationship and ornery sexual and creative tension with Amanda, and downright confronting all the fear, insecurity, and shame within myself that I had to deal with if I was going to grow into a healthier, more self-aware person. It brought to my attention how much of my self-worth was wrapped up in my drumming and also feeling accepted as a person. This time period started me thinking about how to take full personal accountability for my own quality of my life. That as logical or easy as it could seem to blame outside factors, the more direct way to address the problem was to change from within.

By the time we returned in early August from our trip to Japan, I was climaxing in a terrible existential crisis. Anger and frustration, had turned to sadness, then to despair. I wanted to kill myself and was spending enough time thinking about suicide that I knew where and how I was going to do it. There was the constant, stinging sensation that felt like I was the butt end of some kind of twisted joke. That somewhere, some higher power was looking down on me, choking with laughter at the muddled sucker staring another dead end in the face, just when he thought he'd found a way out of the maze. I started suffering sever panic attacks, a crushing depression and in mid-August finally checked myself into St. Elizabeth's Hospital to get help. In addition going to therapy, I decided to back out of a short run of dates that we had scheduled overseas to get

photo by: Amanda Palmer

some time away and get my head straight. It was decided that Amanda would go and do some shows in Scotland solo, which at that time, was a new and unusual situation for us. But, I knew that if I didn't take care of myself then I would be in terrible shape for the recording session and life in general and well, what kind of option is that? So, I got some good counseling and time to think a lot of things through. By the time we ready to go to Allaire, I felt like I was in a place where I could really give the kind of energy to the performances I wanted to deliver.

They were very challenging times to say the least, but I made it through and came out stronger in the end. I taught me a lot about myself and I'm very thankful to the support system of people around me who helped me out and shared their perspectives on things. I'm proud of the work we all did on Yes, Virginia and No, Virginia and love playing in The Dresden Dolls no matter what. Even at its toughest points, if you love the music you make, that's what sustains you. Many times in life, I feel like it's all I've had to get me through. I live to play, it's about as simple as that. Never have I felt so able to express myself through music, as connected to another person on stage as I have playing with Amanda. The music we play and the bond we share as friends has helped me grow stronger as performer and as an individual in ways I'm very grateful for. And I suppose as in music, as in life; the deeper you listen to others and to yourself, the more you learn, and the more eloquently you can respond.

MRS. O.

1st ph - find stronger - less pitchy one↓

Falling→snow bad match

└ which won't send you ORGAN good but
   BOTH CHORUSES.   CUT in drops completely

└ bring savage clovers" organ ↓ subtler

shakes our faith - organ OUT or WAY down

"YOU!" -up
   (can't stop)

→ ‖‖‖‖‖‖‖ - is there one that lasts? [Find.]

MM.

[needs intro]. BAD.

"presently" - up vox

"when they keep" - "

1st ARP - bring [1st note piano arp] in louder - overall louder

"Retinas" - UP - drums are overpowering piano!
                    esp in this verse.
                              esp. KICK.

"YES! everything..." - UP

"soul gets sold" ↗ - punchier. piano UP!

piano sounds LAME
            useless - BASS - piano out of nowhere →

face your...

"selfies?" - search - weak ending....   —

drums are totally overpowering ending —

                need better ending

DB.

(1) "pick a number" - back effect (2) AP: 1st guttoral re-do

2nd/3rd? (3) just "poster B, v1" - Ø harmony (4) "shes" - (1) too abrupt

(5) end too long - put in almost immed. pedal lift.

BACKSTABB

(1) Piano - no extra o'dubs
It's casio + toy piano - or mixdown until "no night?
~~less~~ hihat

(2) bring in Brox in 1st chorus more grad (3) bring drums up at end? not that enough
Kill - something at ~~sun still~~ beginning to announce laugh is awesome
end harmonies not quite so hi
esp imaginary funerals. - Coda: not nuts about knowing elvis vox
~~Sx changes~~
1st snare hit much bigger - missing vox! snare
tick tock piano ↓
ah ah ah ah - effect - separated - a little lower? (1)
piano + drums come in stronger after 1st tomorrow... (or bring down tomorrows...)
vox | cutting | "1"   1st big T+T chorus (pre boys bridge) - move ♡ panning!
Alk last tomorrows... more bass piano/basic synth (hearing way to much OD)
Falling over > (bass run) PIANO louder | very horse? | Vrox
1st (1) basic piano louder in general (3) OD's are overpowering verse 3 mying hard vox Ø lost
"1" chorus comes in weak   "3 wires" sound not good - lost. "ter" not + more piercing - too dull boost
end of solo: don't emphasize overdubs setting's
SING (1) guitar "sing" < stronger delivery shorter - just sounds weak.
(2) there is this thing. slg cos its obvious - add organ? - grow it more (re-do? check)
"life" is no... lost   ah...ah... sound too much like two people singing w/ a chorus effect. LAME. organ out?
need MORE
nrs. falling snow - match this? want sky (3) organ cut in drops > shakes guitar shall not end
w/ piano slam

ger pretty as a picture of a patient on a fresh iv
of sutres where his magic johnson ought to be

need to be the next big thing
elligence and zest ~~for experimenting~~
out the back and keep your mouth shut
no sweat ive got aim like a mack truck
how many more i can fit there
know miss guessing gets you nowhere

emy

powdering the drummer

✓ ANGRY
✓ ✓ WWW @ — luddite/corporate satire
✓ ⊘ SEX @ sex/mast ✓
✓ ✓ EVIL @ — nonsense (luddite) ✓

✓ ⊘ SHIRES @ universal sex song ✓

SATIRICAL ✓
✓ ✓ MRS. O — denial of history ✓
✓ ✓ KILL @ — fuck you ✓
✓ ✓ DIRTY — fuck you ✓
✓ ✓ B-STAB @ — fuck you ✓
⊘ MANDY — Back alley dancer ✓
✓ ✓ ALK @ alchol/lonliness ✓

SAD
✓ ✓ SINS @ — universal makeup call
✓ BOSTON — relationship song ✓
✓ ORG @ sex/mast/lonliness ⊘
⊘ MIN @ lonliness/alcohol ⊘
✓ ✓ DELILAH — sex/loneliness ✓
⊘ GARDENER — sex/fear ⊘

71

photo by: Emily White

photo by: Emily White

Amanda's Bedroom

Brian's Bedroom

ONE Day,
WE WENT FoR a WALK
it was awesome.

for.

photo by: Brian Viglione

photo by: Amanda Palmer

photo by assistant engineer: matt snedecor

photo by: Amanda Palmer

one day, I became moderately stir-crazy

Amanda Self Portrait

photo by: Emily White

Paul as Jefferson

photo by: Kelly Davidson

photo by: Sheri Hausey

95

photo by: Sheri Hausey

photo by: Sheri Hausey

photo by: Sheri Hausey

producer Sean Slade, international man of mystery

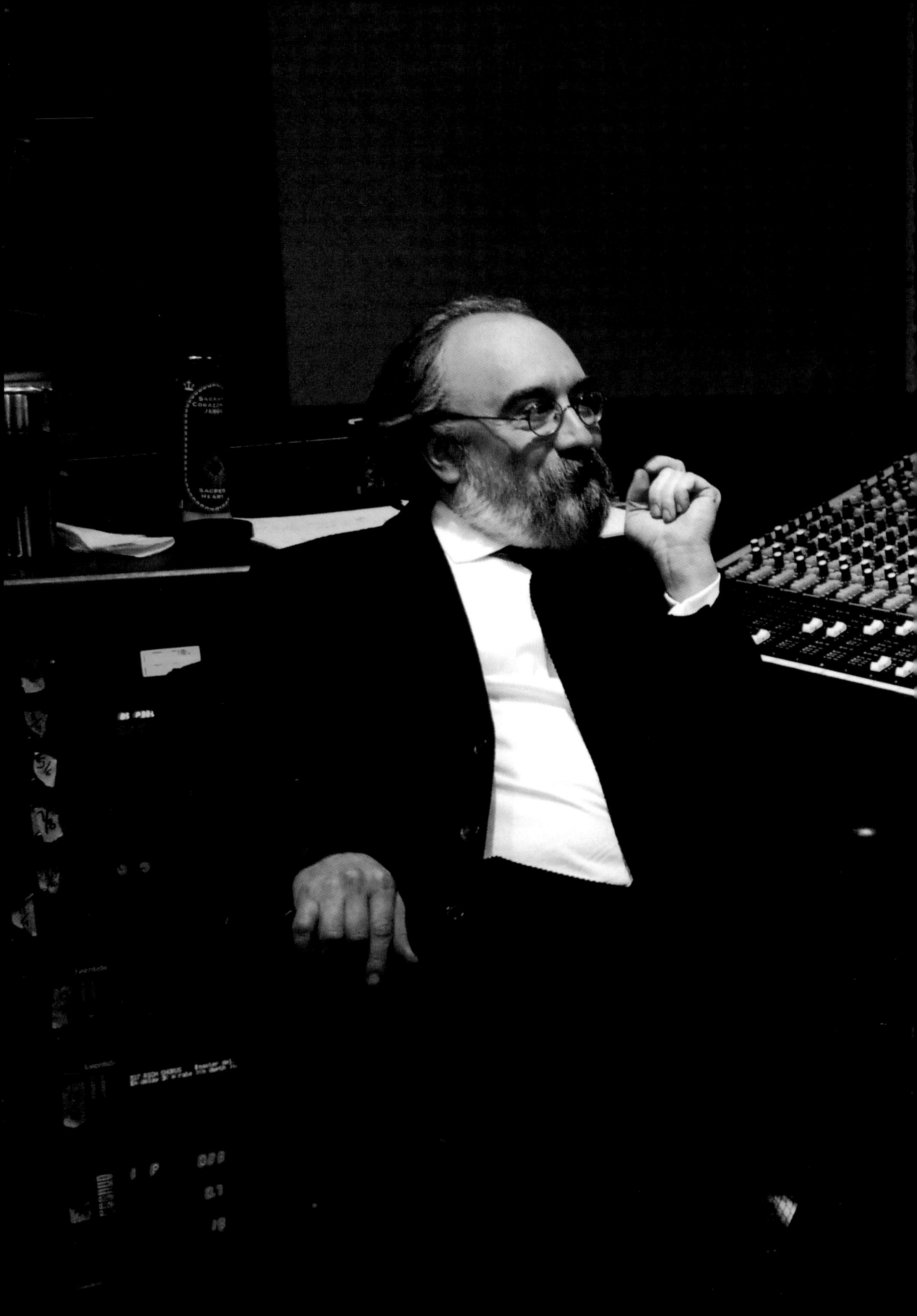

photo by: Sheri Hausey

photo by: Sheri Hausey

ABOUT THE ARTWORK

The initial artwork ideas for Yes, Virginia went through a bunch of different incarnations.

My original idea was to have Barnaby Whitfield (a brilliant, brilliant artist who had done the Paradise DVD cover and our "Good Day" 7" cover) create a cover and possibly some artwork for each song. We went through rounds of ideas for the cover, including a surreal Norman Rockwell knock-off, but it was impossible for all three of us (Barnaby, Brian & I) to approve any ONE image. We ended up using Barnaby's iconic WWII propaganda-style portraits on the two inside flaps of the digipak, and I consoled myself with the fact that his unused work would be displayed in full-color glory in the sheet music book (Ta Da).

Meanwhile, I wanted to include art made by our friends and fans, since we'd been getting such a tremendous number of good submissions (unbidden) through the website. So I posted an email searching for any images inspired by "Backstabber," "Me & the Minibar," "Mrs. O," "First Orgasm," "Sex Changes," "Mandy Goes to Med School" and "Delilah," since these were the songs that were already circulating on the net as live versions. We got hundreds of submissions and Emily White and the Ninja Interns at Madison House spent hours meticulously filing them and emailing them to me (I was on tour most of this time) for inspection.

I wondered how to fit the submitted art into the booklet; just laying the art on a black background seemed boring. Barnaby and I discussed trying to make the booklet read like a children's story, with a little Virginia walking through hallways of a twisted museum or a gallery. At this same time, synchronicity sent me a burned disc of photos in the mail, taken by my old friend Nicholas Vargelis. Nick and I had been crossing paths for years; he's lived at my house, done lighting for the band and designed lights for a handful of plays that I've directed, including "Hotel Blanc." One of his passions is urban exploration, which is a fancy way of saying he breaks into crumbling old buildings, lights the space and takes pictures. There was a beautiful old theater in Boston—unused since the 1920s or so—called The Gaiety. It was, despite community attempts to preserve it, about to be wrecking-balled to make way for condos. Nick took a whole series of illicit photos a few weeks before the building was demolished and sent me the shots on disc, thinking I might have some use for them. My brain snapped into place and those photos became the backdrop for the artwork.

art by: Barnaby Whitfield

photo by brian viglion

making the heartplane logo in the back bus lounge
on the NIN tour....

The criteria for the submitted images that I ended using in the booklet came down to a combination of how well the piece matched the song and how well it sat within the framework of Nick's beautiful photos of decay. In some cases ("Delilah", "Mandy" and "Modern Moonlight") we managed to take several pieces of art and hang them in one setting. Mark Berger was the Photoshop master who made this all possible. I would send him the background and the submitted art that I had chosen, along with some loose guidelines about how to set up the entire scene. Then he would charge forward, often adding his own imaginative elements. Since he was doing the layout design for the entire package—on top of also maintaining the Dolls website—we probably exchanged no less than 1500 emails within a period of a few months. I thank him elsewhere in this book, but I must again stand and applaud this man for his extreme tenacity and patience.

As for the cover: after the Barnaby paintings were set aside and we were searching for other options, I got very excited about this old picture of my mother from a New Jersey photo booth. God only knows what she was thinking when she took it. I think she was just trying to be dramatic (and I didn't relate at alllll, not a bit). I had been hanging onto this photo assuming it would, someday, have the perfect purpose. Mark and I mocked up a bunch of different covers using the photo, but at some point somebody (I don't remember whether it was Brian or management or someone at the label) wasn't nuts about it. So I manically changed tactics and started getting excited about the idea of using the heart-plane logo I'd drawn (which, by the by, was not even supposed to be used for the band: it was supposed to be the logo for Post-War Trade, a concept company of fan-made Dolls merchandise). Everybody seemed to agree that this was a good idea, so we started mocking it up. My memory and Brian's memory get very hazy around this point. I remember being in the loud in-between-cars spot of a European train on a conference call with four people about the record cover, since we were hours away from deadline. Everybody disagreed about this color and that border and this image and I took the phone away from my head, stared at the trees blurring by and thought: When did this become such a disaster? At the end of the day, the final cover was approved by everybody and truly liked by (as far as I can deduce) nobody. I still hope we can re-release the record at some point with the cover in silver and black. It was a valuable lesson in how easy it is to get artistically knocked off track by a committee. Committees and art = bad mix.

A few odds and ends:

The colored-pencil stained-glass Virginia on the back of the booklet is one of my favorite images; it was created by Zea Barker, a.k.a. Bony Lil, another long-time Dolls collaborator, and inspired by "Mrs. O."

The beautiful collage behind the disc tray came from E. Stephen Frederick, a fine friend of mine who also supplied us with the wonderful dollhouse-in-rubble image for the first record. Thanks go to him and the Empire S.N.A.F.U. archives from which his work was culled.

If you watch Michael Pope's alternate cut of the "Sing" video on the internet, you'll catch a few references to the Gaiety Theater being destroyed.

Cover mock-ups by Mark Berger

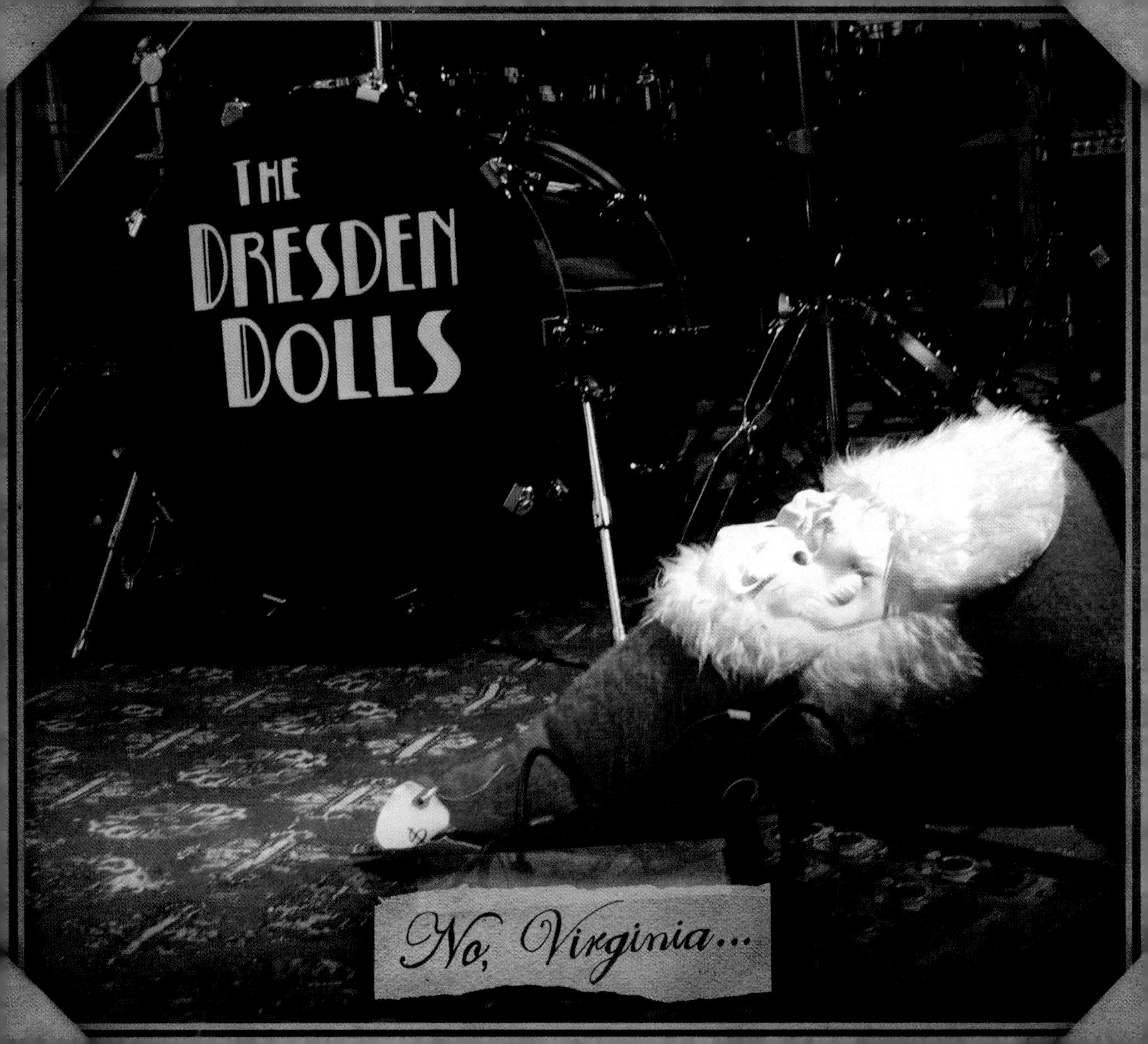
THE
DRESDEN
DOLLS
No, Virginia...

modern moonlight presenting modern moonlight just as advertised coke and pepsi finally found a compromis
est bidder then they turn around and merger and they merger and the merger and they murder and they murd
light presenting modern moonlight just as advertised coke and pepsi finally found a compromise how can
old to the highest bidder then they turn around and merger and they merger and the merger and they mu
is over you can read the paper

YOUR AD HERE

yes! everything is absolutely making sense… every time you turn around your soul gets sold to the high
ourself for miracles you're in for a nasty shock when the war is over you can read the paper modern moonl
magnificence! yes! everything is absolutely making sense… every time you turn around your soul gets s
htrope walker boys and girls brace yourself for miracles you're in for a nasty shock when the war

face yourself wire cutters of the world you know what to use it for spread the word to all the tig
e cynic in me god I love communicating! I just hate the shit we're missing… everybody join in the
world you know what to use it for spread the word to all the word to use it for spread the world and girls brace y
nic in me god I love communicating! I just hate the shit we're missing… everybody oin in the magnific

complain that we're all fucked up kids when they keep on changing who our mother is? (like it all you wa
who murders most will take it all...... (fight it all you want it's useless night is in the way of progres
hat we're all fucked up kids when they keep on changing who our mother is? (like it all you want it'
murder and the one who murders most will take it all...... (fight it all you want it's useless night is

nt it's fruitless night is in the way of progress) retinas are bleeding for the enterprise surgically wired i
s) we're gonna take your cities one by one cut your cables cut your cords and spoil all your fun we're gon
s fruitless night is in the way of progress) retinas are bleeding for the enterprise surgically wired t
in the way of progress) we're gonna take your cities one by one cut your cables cut your cords and

spoil all your fun we re gonna make your light cos stripped of your equipment you ll
nto paradise yesterday I dropped in on the MKB everyone was messaging like it was going out of style
na make your light a living hell cos stripped of your equipment you ll be forced to face yourself wire
nto paradise yesterday I dropped in on the MKB everyone was messaging like it was going out of style it w

Mock-up for Modern Moonlight by Mark Berger

E. Stephen Frederick, with thanks to the Empire S.N.A.F.U. Archives.

the artwork of BARNABY WHITFIELD

photoshop collage for potential painting

Unfinished Modern Moonlight with collage

The SHORES of CALIFORNIA

sketch by Barnaby Whitfield

Barnaby Whitfield

Barnaby Whitfield

Some Clown

Yes, Virginia

Barnaby Whitfield

Barnaby Whitfield

"Virginia?"

Barnaby Whitfield

VIRGINIA

art by Zea Barker

fuji Rock.
Art. Work. Art. Work. Artwor
Artwork Artwork Art work
work. Art. Art. Work. Work.
2:28. Waiting until Luka calls
due Just the ground to c
Ahhhhhhhhhhhhhhhhh
Shhh

MUSIC

Notes for the player...

Sex Changes

When I was in my early-to-mid twenties, I briefly dated a very pretty boy who was—I soon found out—weeks away from going under the knife to become a girl. We never became that close, but the timing of it all was certainly bizarre. I was meeting him in his last few moments of being Him and there were long letters from the hospital that seeped into my own ongoing inquiry of relationships, gender, identity and about how Sex Changes Everything. I was also feeling the first creeping horror—even though I was swinging and single—of the Baby Conundrum that women in their mid-twenties slowly start to face. (No Choice is still a Choice, unfortunately.) That creeping seeped its way into the song. So did abortion. Abortion is so inspiring!

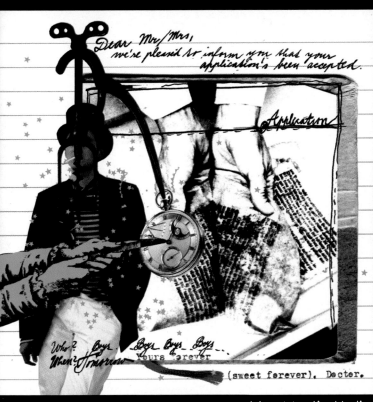

art by Martin Hrdina

art by Kaley McKean

art by Janet Bruesselbach

art by Suzie Am

SEX CHANGES

Someone once posted online—or wrote to me, I can't remember—that they were upset because this song seemed anti-transgender. This is not true. I'm as anti-sex-reassignment as I am anti-abortion or, for that matter, anti-sex (which is to say, not at all.) This doesn't mean I never spend time musing about the pros, cons and, most of all, the emotional aftershocks.

Sex reassignment, losing your virginity, abortion, Getting It On in general....oh, how liberating to have the choice to do these things! And yet how mortally terrifying should you ever regret the decisions you make.

Note for the Player: This song is good for banging large portions of the piano with your arm.

art by Nura Tafech

art by Emy Koopman

SEX CHANGES

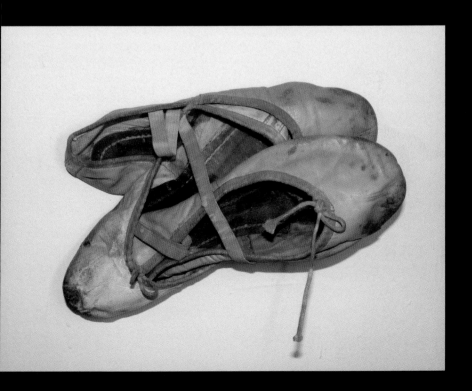

art by Sarah Beetson

art by Sheri Demchak

127

Backstabber

I often get asked Who this song is about. At the end of the day it's not fair to assign it to a specific person; as with most of my songs, it's far too exaggerated to pin on something and/or someone too specific.

art by Chris Kisler

art by Stefa

BACKSTABBER

It was first inspired by a dinner conversation I was having with a friend who was also a local musician. At the time, Our Band was just barely clawing our way out of Boston, but we were charging forth, touring a lot, making a name, finding fans, feeling excited and inspired. We were teeming with optimism. We were working ourselves to the bone and were convinced that we'd succeed on a bigger level. I asked my friend, as I lifted a bite of seaweed salad to my mouth: "What do you think? Do you think we'll make it?"

In retrospect, this was a stupid question to ask. I knew the answer I wanted to hear and hearing anything else was just bound to upset me and burst my little bubble. I asked anyway, probably because I thought I was going to get the nice, juicy, ego-watering answer I deserved (which would have been, of course: "Are you going to MAKE IT, Amanda? Of course you shall! Why, you're going to achieve unimaginable heights of glory and happiness through your magnificent songwriting and compelling stage presence! And the DRUMMER! So handsome, so talented! You Go Girl!!!!!")

This was not the answer I got. The answer I got, after he pondered a moment over a futomaki roll, was "I half-expect you'll succeed."

It pissed me off. But his off-hand comment was only one moment, a small, insignificant drop in the bucket. He was, in fact, generally supportive. Nevertheless, the comment stung like hell and kept ringing in my head. The whole music scene was bringing me down at the time with all of its "who-the-fuck-do-you-think-you-are" attitude. Everybody wanted success, but felt compelled to hoard their enthusiasm and optimism for their own bands and projects. It seemed, sometimes, like nobody wanted to be happy for us.

The Noise Board was an online discussion forum where it was at the time very in vogue amongst jaded Boston musicians to discuss the awfulness of The Dresden Dolls. I, being an unlucky combination of vain and masochistic (like most performers) wasn't able to pry myself away from reading these endless rants about how Our Band was talentless, schticky, doomed, unshaven, lame and—simply put—SO GAY. I took some amount of pride in it, trying to believe in the age-old adage that the opposite of hate is indifference and all that jazz. Let's not forget our Oscar Wilde: the only thing in life worse than being talked about is not being talked about. But, of course, it still hurt like hell.

In the Nice Twist of Fate Dept., it was this same dinner-comment-friend who, upon hearing my grumbling admission to reading the daily pummeling the band was taking on the internet, literally smacked me out of my daze and said "AMANDA, STOP." And stop I did (well, more or less. I still peek in for the occasional beating, but find to my dismay that their venom is now generally reserved for other local bands, so my masochistic self has to haul over to the Hate Mail section of our website or read outdated Bad Press, which just isn't as satisfying...though I can just Google "hate Dresden Dolls" if I want to get a decent fix.) I don't think I've ever properly thanked him for that.

art by Joshua A. Camarco

art by Gecedille

Brian's Notes for Drumming: Rhythmically, the drums and piano work together almost identically.
They accent and rest together, add inflection on certain lines (ex. "shut your mouth and fight me"), but mostly provide a comfortable foundation for the... benevolent narrator.
Improvise your own maniacal laugh at the end, as you feel it.

Modern Moonlight

This is one of the older ones: I wrote it when I was 22, around the same time I wrote "Half Jack."

I was daydreaming one day about how long it was going to take before someone figured out how to post billboards on the moon, and I went off on a little joke in my head about how Coke and Pepsi would probably vie for the spot. Then I started wondering who would win. Then I started thinking how funny it would be if they just followed the cycle of the moon and traded off every 28 days or so.

At the same time, I was trying to keep up my classical piano chops by practicing the third movement of Beethoven's "Moonlight Sonata." It was one of a handful of Impressive-Sounding-Pieces-Of-Classical-Music that I knew by heart. I'd been trying to learn it (by ear) since high school and had finally set myself to the task of learning it (by sight-reading) in college. For about a month in 1996, I could play the whole thing from memory. Once I stopped practicing it frequently, I lost it completely. But like the first lines of poems and speeches we know so well, I can still play the first 30 seconds of that thing cold. So there I was in my freezing Somerville apartment, several years later, trying to play the first 30 seconds of the third movement of the Moonlight Sonata on my electric keyboard and trying to feel like a real piano player instead of a lazy bohemian slacker with no motivation or future (and failing, I should add, on both counts). In addition to these things, I was thinking about how the world was becoming more and more superficially connected and—from my point of view—didn't seem all that much happier as a result. If you listen to that third movement,

art by Pana Stamos

MODERN

art by Alec Johnson, S. Adrienne Elder, Chelsea Shanno

art by Chris Kisler

the Beethoven quote should appear obvious. I recommend the Philips Edition with Alfred Brendel on piano.

Somewhere in the closet there is an old four-track version of this song that I recorded in that cold apartment with all of the original lyrics. They morphed quite a bit over the years. (In 1998, as I recall, there was no text messaging.)

Note for the Player: If you can't play the fast part very well, don't worry. I can't play it either. I overdubbed it onto the record and I think I've played it flawlessly live once or twice (out of a few hundred concerts).

MOONLIGHT

art by Chiara Ambrosio

Brian's Notes for Drumming:
There are three songs that I realized channeled for this song; "My War" by Black Flag, "Demanufacture" by Fear Factory, and "Suicide Note Pt. 2" by Pantera. Mom will be so proud. The whole middle is just playing off accenting the words and Amanda's inflection. The big swells at the end should make it seem as if every power-line and transformer on your block is simultaneously exploding every laptop, microwave, cell phone and television on your block and taking us all out in the process.

My Alcoholic Friends

They say that you are every character in your own dreams. I assume the same can be applied to songwriting. I love my drunk friends the way I love my drunk self—with a sloshy combination of love, disgust and concern.

Brian's Notes for Drumming: Get a solid comfortably paced backbeat happening here and SWING IT! Don't be afraid to dig in where it needs it, layback where it doesn't. This one has to swagger down the street like it's had a few too many sips of the bubbly.

DELILAH

Delilah

I was recently given the opportunity to write a short piece for an excellent Buddhist magazine called Shambhala Sun, and this is what I wrote.

When they ran it, they titled it "Melody vs. Meditation" and they asked me for a graphic, so I made them a sharpie drawing of me eating my own head.

When I sit on certain days, I do not have a hard time letting go of films, grudges and grocery lists. But I can't let go of music. A song is Different. A song has special status, doesn't it? Let me clarify: not a pre-existing jingle floating around in there, but a true glimmer of inspiration, a little tuneful embryo waiting to be born into a full-fledged ballad. A Really Good Idea. I am a songwriter; I need these moments bad.

As an artist, I've unwittingly prioritized my life to keep the radio-receiver of my head tuned to a clear inspirational frequency; braced to receive brilliant and clever ideas at any moment. This has, however, also seemed to mean being an impractical idiot,

art by Sheena Antoinette Seago

admiring the beauty, poetry and irony of the piano about to fall on my head instead of getting out of the goddamn way.

The songwriter in me struggles like mad when meditating. The rules of my conditioned art-mind say: Nothing must stand in the way of a developing idea. When inspiration calls, I follow. If I should be struggling with ANYTHING in my life, it should be that impossibly disciplined step from thought to pen to paper, from line-sung-into-cell-phone to sitting at piano, from seed to full song.

I watch this mental boxing match take place with interest. In one corner sits a meditator, who calmly suggests that good ideas will linger if they are worth a damn. And so what if they don't? The songs are not happening, only sitting is happening. In the other corner paces the crazed composer with the mind that has been specifically cultivated to jump from image to word and from image to melody in an effort to create a work of art that will move her fellow humans. A perfect song is a captured moment of inspiration barely touched. When a good idea hits, it's as if you've thrown a set of colored juggling balls in the air and taken a blurred —yet beautiful—photograph. If I have the patience to develop that photo unaltered, I will have a perfect song. Often I am convinced that I can get a better photo through sheer willpower and hard work (just a LITTLE better! a bit lighter, a bit darker there, no wait....!). This is where meditating and art-making go hand in hand. Spending hour after hour laboring on finding the perfect line or the perfect arrangement of notes is about as productive as mindlessly wandering the world seeking the perfect-looking tree under which you'll find enlightenment.

I was on silent retreat at the Insight Meditation Center in Barre some years ago. The air was just beginning to carry that sugary spring scent, the rot of winter leftovers melting up from the dampening ground. Away from the city, no tangles of pipe and concrete between me and the crust of the earth. Just my feet, taking steps; my eye adjusting in the light; my nose taking in the thaw; my mind... hooked on a beautiful melody that floated into my head that I was trying desperately to ignore and trying desperately to continue.

There's no end

To the love

You can give

When you change your point of view

To underfoot

The best songs come like this, the melody and the words landing on the brain's sunny afternoon kitchen table like a singing telegram, a complete and precise little package of information. In that telegram is encoded the entire blueprint for the verses and chorus, a musical strand of DNA. I cannot recognize the words, the length, or even the subject of the song, but I can detect something about how the song will feel when finished. I've always suspected that this glimpse of the whole from the part offers an excellent metaphor for life and death in general.

The problem with meditation is that it unlocks the door to inspiration, I thought, and the problem with me is that I am in love with my own inspiration.

art by Die Booth

The match was on and the artist, as far as I could tell, knocked out the meditator with a single left hook. I let the singing in my head continue on at full volume (I think I even let it out of my mouth occasionally and scared some squirrels) until I returned, at which point I broke my non-writing-and-reading vows and jotted the whole song down; a song now called "Delilah" which wound up being a key track on my band's last album, barely edited from that moment. I always felt a little bit of guilty pleasure in the birth of that song, as if I'd gotten away with committing some spiritual heist.

I shared this anecdote with a friend and he pointed out that creativity isn't necessarily an obstacle to meditation but rather its fruit. Only now, several years later, do I realize the obvious. The moment of divine inspiration may certainly strike at any time. The true meditation is to have the power and clarity to decide when, where, how and even if we want to be struck.

(Originally published in Shambhala Sun, May 2008. Reprinted with kind permission.)

I must add this piece of information since I have been asked on frequent occasions: There isn't actually a Denny's on Route 1 (though it is home to a bunch of strip joints and the infamous Hilltop Steak House which has lots of life-size plastic cows and cacti out front—if you're in Boston, check it out). But to say "Denny's on Bedford Street near the Bedford/Lexington border" didn't fit. And that's the Denny's I was thinking about when I wrote this.

Sheena Antoinette Seago, Die Booth, Emy Koopman, Leila Marlene von Meyer

art by Annette E. Padilla

Brian's Notes for Drumming: The drums are basically a sparse pulse in the verse, kind of lonely feeling. The choruses are like knocking back that shot of gin and getting smacked across the face for not knowing better. There's a two hit set up on the floor toms at the end of the "oh oh" section with a crash to act as painful 1,2,3 combo. Let's see how fast this thing can go? Start the engine with the snare roll and then pop the clutch and punch it. There's nothin' but open road in front of you and your playing, double time now, leaving that sack of shit boyfriend to rot in that no good town behind you. Every snare hit is another exit sign you just passed on the highway. The sun's coming up over the horizon and you're not stopping until the tank's empty.

Dirty Business

This one lives, thematically, with "Backstabber," though it was written a few years earlier. I was filled with a weird brand of vitriol for a few years there and, with no recent breakup providing a handy target, I turned to whatever else was making me angry.

White Suburban Girl Guilt dies hard.

At the time, there was a collection of checkout girls at Pearl Art & Craft Supplies on Massachusetts Avenue. I wanted them to like me.

<u>Brian's Notes for Drumming:</u> This song seems to have 4 parts to it; the main verse, the "To all the ones…" parts, the "She's the kind of girl.." sections, and the turnaround with the random shouting. Main verses are played heavily on the floor tom and snare and accent/ answer the same rhythm as the piano part. "To all the ones…" comes down to an eighth note pulse and is essentially a segue section. The turn around section is 3 bars of 4/4 and a bar of 2/4. After several failed attempts on my part in the studio to shout anything random that sounded "good", it was Sean Slade who suggested that I shout "Mishima" in time with the music. This was of course a nod to Yukio Mishima, the acclaimed Japanese playwright and poet, who committed seppuku after giving a speech intended to start coup d' etat. However you may interject any historical figure or gibberish of your choice.

FIRST ORGASM

First Orgasm

This song is a based on a true story.

One thing I loved about the album art entries for this song was their strikingly similar composition. I choose, for this reason, to include many of them for your enjoyment (and maybe they will make you uncomfortable, or—better yet—turn you on, or—better still—strip you of the illusion that girls don't whack off while home alone when procrastinating at their laptops).

It was fascinating to me when we started playing this song live;

art by Lisa Tagliaferri

art by Nan Baker

art by Tim Youster

art by Claire Cant

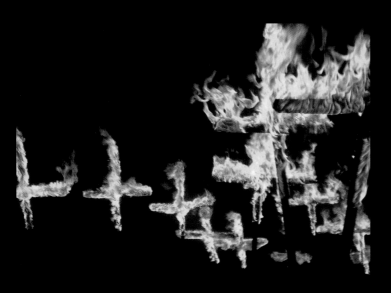

art by Claire Cant

art by Remi Enge

would go totally one way or the other. The third or fourth time we played it live, the audience laughed throughout the entire first and second verses. The song IS incredibly funny (though depressing as hell). There's an interesting confusion that happens to audiences when they are struck with the Vulgar, the Intimately Personal and the Very Sad all at the same time. I wish there was a word for it, because I fall into this trap all the time.   For the most part, I enjoy it immensely. Maybe it should just be called Art.

art by Sarah Beetsont

Brian's Notes for Drumming: This is one of those blurry, interpretive songs. I guess the feeling behind the big build up at the end is just the same as when your feeling kind of down and alone and you think to yourself, "Aha, I know what I'll do to make myself feel better" and its not Eat Chocolate or Look at Funny-Cute Cat Videos on the Internet, either. So there you are with yourself and your going for it, trying to block out that shitty, aching in your chest as best as you can. You're trying to focus on anything other than how empty you feel and you're scrambling to find something hot to think about. Then you start to well up and 3, 2, 1, ahhhh, and just after you hit that critical point of release, you're struck with that wave of total, pathetic, humiliation and you sit there, with yourself in your hand, tears running down your face, feeling about 100 times worse than you did before. Take that scene and put the cymbal swell accents on the 1 and the "and" of 4.

art by Helen Nehill

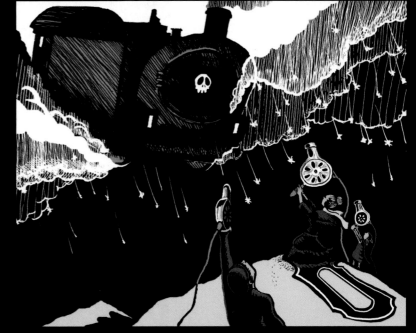

Zachary Shiff
• www.myspace.com/4therecorddesigns

MRS. O.

Mrs. O.

My stepfather John's mother lived in Lexington (where I was raised) and died when I was about 14 years old. We were never very close, but she was a sort of grandmother-by-proxy. Her last name was Oberteuffer, which none of us kids could pronounce, so we called her "Mrs. O".

It was her age and the rhythmic quality of her name that spawned this tune more than anything specifically about her. She always seemed like a distant ghost of some far off generation. I remember starting the doo-wop riff for this song and having "O Mrs. O" just pop right in there because it fit so well. The rest of the song just came out in a confused jumble of things my brain had been recently chewing on.

I was in the process of workshopping a collectively written play called "Hotel Blanc," which examined how the Holocaust echoed through three generations of a family, their stories morphing and overlapping in space and time. We were tackling the Big Questions about our inherited perceptions of "lies" and "truth." I was a German studies major in college and spent a lot of time thinking about the Holocaust and its aftermath.

One thing that inspired that play—and this song—was something one of my German-born professors said to me before I moved to Germany in 1996. She had been raised in the 1950s, when Germany was in a collectively-devastated post-war shellshock. She told me that NOBODY discussed the war, the Holocaust, Hitler...not a word, nothing, none of it. It wasn't taught in school, it wasn't transmitted to her from her parents. It was just too harrowing and everybody zippered up into a superficial veneer to survive the trauma until the truth gradually started leaking out when the country was ready.

art by Dustin Parker

Potential Walmart-safe alternative

MRS. O.

Shortly thereafter, when I was living in Germany, I started piecing together the fact that my professor was exactly my mother's age and that the majority of my friends (mostly born in the '70s) were raised by parents who had been brought up in this emotional vacuum. And the consequence of that on THEIR personalities was...loud and strange.

It was hard to explain in words, less hard to explain in art.

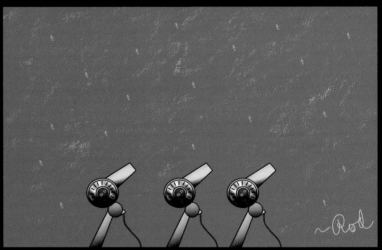

art by Roderick Chauncey

Brian's Notes for Drumming: The initial inspiration for this feel came from a mix of the Beatles' song, "Oh, Darling", from Abbey Road, and "Mother" by John Lennon from the first Plastic Ono Band record.   Not that Mrs. O really sounds like either one of those songs, but I liked the power in the sparseness of the drumming on those songs. If you listen to them, you might see what I was going for. I like a lot of the lifts and nuances in Mrs. O that always makes it a fun one to perform live.   The dynamic (volume) of the song is constantly fluctuating according to what's happening in the narrative as well.

Shores of California

It must have been sometime in my mid-twenties when I realized the full impact of the male sex drive vs. the female emotional drive.

But as I now say: we have to deal with PMS and they have to deal with often unwanted erections. Maybe it's a fair trade. Not much we can do about it, unless you want to refer back to song #1.

I faced a struggle with the line "that's the way Aristophanes and Homer wrote The Iliad and Lysistrada." I tried turning it around to be correct, because, in reality, Aristophanes wrote the Lysistrada (a Greek comedy about how the wives of the men refused to have sex with them during the Peloponnesian war until peace was declared. Good Move!) and Homer wrote the Iliad (the much bloodier epic poem follow-up to The Odyssey which chronicles the further dramas resulting from the Trojan War—which was set into motion by the world's most famous and history-altering Jealous Husband) but it just didn't fit. I tried to work in a back-up vocal that cried "NOT IN THAT ORDER" for a while but that didn't work either and would have made a lyric that was already super-fucking pretentious even more super-fucking pretentious. So I left it. But if anyone asks, I did not misinform you. Homer = Iliad. Aristophanes = Lysistrada. Ok.

SHORES of CALIFORNIA

Brian's Notes for Drumming: The verse of this song is actually a beat that I lifted from a Karen Mantler song called, "I'm His Boss" that Amanda and I used to cover years ago. The drummer plays this kind of inverted bossa-nova beat, where the down beat gets pushed by an eighth note, so that the snare accent is not on 2 and 4, but on the "and" of 2 and the "and" of 4. The chorus beat is basically "We're Not Gonna Take It" by Twisted Sister. So there you have it, knock yourself out.

art by Pat Maguire

art by Zoe B. Kraus

Necessary Evil

Necessary Evil is the cousin complaint to Modern Moonlight, featuring my fictional Luddite fraternity of One. This song definitely holds the record for enduring the greatest number of drafts and rewrites. In the end, I don't think a single lyric remained from the very first version of this song (around 1999) to when I finished it (in 2005—in the studio right before we recorded it).

"Luddite fraternity of One"? WTF does that mean?

I talked about this in the last songbook: usually the songs that come fast and whole are the most meaningful. This one is a pieced together collage of variations on a theme, as if the pages of a diary were thrown in the air and then pieced back together in random order. There was an entire version of song where I sang "I've gone from speech to text" instead of the words "and take your Listerine."

Where Listerine actually came from I'm not sure, but it certainly turned into a pain in the ass when it came to titling the song, because we found out that it's technically a copyright infringement to use a Brand Name as a Song Title (supposedly lyrics within the song are okay) though I have no idea if that's actually true given the number of existing songs titles featuring "Cadillac." In any event, Necessary Evil won second prize.

Brian's Notes for Drumming: This was a fun song to work on because it has rapid changes, and a fun variation on a common rhythmic pattern in Amanda's writing, and an exciting, driving tempo at about 186 bpm. Keeping straight sixteenth notes through this whole tune is a good work out. There's a certain syncopated rhythm that Amanda frequently uses in her writing which is to use the accents 1 and 2 and 3 and 4 and. It has a great sense of persistence and urgency to it and helps drive the beat forward. I decided to break it up by alternating every other accent between the kick and side stick on the snare, as opposed to play "kick, kick, snare- kick, kick, snare" like on Half Jack or Girl Anachronism. Its not drastic, but I liked how it sounded. The choruses explode out of the gate and the beat stays pretty unrelenting from the solo through the end of the song.

art by Edward Cao

art by Jenny Gonzale

art by Holly Hutchings

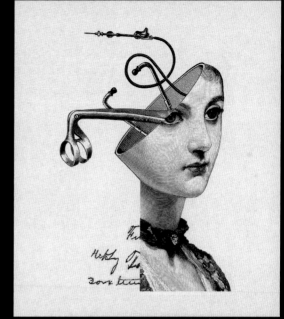

art by Claudia Drake

art by Blake Gentry

MANDY GOES TO MED SCHOOL

Mandy Goes to Med School

As I pointed out earlier in the book, abortion is such an inspiring topic! I use this song as a reminder to myself that—like "Coin-Operated Boy" —some of the simplest, yet sickest ideas make the best songs. You just have to let yourself be weird enough to sit down and actually write them.

I was particularly impressed by the artwork submissions that came in for this song —they had the greatest visual and thematic dynamics and some were downright terrifying.

<u>Brian's Notes for Drumming:</u> One of my favorites to play live. It has lots of swing, improvisation, plenty of interaction with Amanda and playing off of each other. It's a song that I would've loved to have seen someone like Louis Armstrong or Fats Waller perform because it lends itself to that kind of humorous interpretation and spontaneity.

art by R.A.Friedman

art by Sadie Marie Mueller

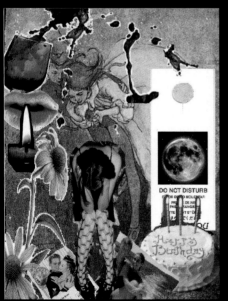

art by CookGilligan

art by Jamie Scandal • www.jamiescandal.com

Me & the Minibar

Not every hotel or motel has a minibar. Sometimes it's a really sad moment when it's the middle of the night and you're done with all you need to do and you draw a bath and you make the bad hotel lighting as non-terrible as possible and you head to the little dorm-sized refrigerator expecting to find 18 ice-cold little friends waiting for you...and there is nobody there.

ME and the MINI-BAR

Brian's Notes for Drumming: Catch breath, sip water, offer moral support to your singer from side of stage.

art by Jessica King

art by Janet Bruesselbach

Sing

I almost never write songs deliberately. But I remember thinking how awesome it would be to write a song with a sing-along-able part that anybody could sing and feel liberated while singing.

So I wrote this.

Then I found out, on tour, that the ending AHHHHH AHHHHHH AHHHH part was completely out of my singing range and it was brutalizing my voice. For a while I took it out of the set because I just hated having to sing it.

Believe me: the irony of this situation did not escape me.

The story comes full circle because nowadays I just pray that the audience will sing it and I can hide behind their voices. Which is kind of beautiful, when you think about it.

Brian's Notes for Drumming: This kicks in with a strong 6/8 feel after the first chorus, but during the second chorus, the kick pattern starts to accent the "and" of 2 and 3 and play off beats on the toms to give it a little more lift. Beautiful song and it should just be soaring by the end of it.

photo by Sheri Hausey

NO VIRGINIA

Dear Jenny

I always loved "Dear Prudence" and that's the one I had in mind when I started writing this. It's a sort of "Dear Prudence" through the psych ward looking-glass.

This is, if you're talking songwriting chronology, one of the oldest songs on the No, Virginia collection. Brian and I used to play this one at our first shows back in 2001, but then we somehow forgot about it. We re-visited working on it for Yes, Virginia but then realized it was too similar to "Backstabber"...so we put it in The Vault.

Like "Necessary Evil," I also re- and re- and redrafted these lyrics. I always feel weird doing that. It feels like cheating somehow. I often find myself being embarrassed by lyrics I wrote when I was younger, they're so...young.

<u>Brian's Notes for Drumming:</u> I was listening to the album "Evil Empire" by Rage Against The Machine a lot around the time we went to record this song at Mad Oak Studios after the January '08 tour. Somehow to me, the beat of their song, "Vietnow" wanted to also find its way into "Dear Jenny" when the beat kicks back in, in the second and third verses, so that's what I went for.

Night Reconnaissance

Ah, the suburbs! The ugly lawn ornaments! The endless possibilities and the giddy randomness of youth!

This song is, if you're again talking songwriting chronology, the newest one of the batch. I wrote it right before we recorded Yes, Virginia and really loved it, but there was, again, a pre-production battle between this song and "My Alcoholic Friends," since the feel was so similar.

When I was working on my solo record, I brought this one to Ben Folds and he, too, loved it, so we tried recording a version of it with his wonderful bassist Jared Reynolds (with Ben on drum duty). We listened to the rough recording several times over the next few days and at one point, Ben turned to me and said "I'm firing myself as the drummer. This is a Dresden Dolls song." So I put it back in my bag and pulled it out for the No, Virginia sessions.

The original lyrics was "hide from the guns," which I then changed to "cunts," which I then decided was too vulgar, so I changed it to "gunts" or "cuns"—whichever I was in the mood for while I was doing the vocal take—so I wouldn't have to decide. I'm still not sure how I'm going to play this one live. I might switch it up every other line.

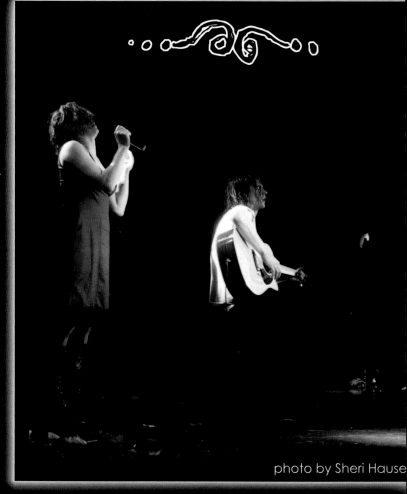

photo by Sheri Hause

<u>Brian's Notes for Drumming:</u> Very straightforward, 4/4-shuffle feel. Lay into it, keep it simple, and keep an eye on the dynamics. The lyrics need to jump out in several spots so pay attention to volume.

The Mouse and the Model

This one is a real oddball. I wrote this and rewrote the lyrics a few dozen times and was still never happy with it. It also has that diary-collage feeling of "Necessary Evil"—I could tell you what each line is about and what inspired it, but I couldn't tell you why they all found their way into the same song.

Trivia Dept.: There was a brief time for a few months in 2003 when we had a guitar player (Greg Disterhoft) and a bass player (Jim Smith, who was then replaced by Andrew DiMola). It was at exactly this time that a then-unfamiliar Sean Slade came to see us play and extended us the invitation to record a song in his studio— "pro bono," as he called it. We booked a few days immediately but weren't really sure what to record. We'd been playing "Good Day" and "Gravity" with Greg and Jim, but those had already been recorded for the first record. So I pulled out "The Mouse and the Model" and another song called "Awful Detail" and we recorded those two. "Awful Detail" didn't turn out so hot, but we were happy as hell with this one.

The vocals were rerecorded when we went to Allaire to record Yes, Virginia, since my voice had really improved in the two-year gap, and we re-mixed it when we mixed the record. It didn't quite fit into the flow, though, and it introduced instruments that wouldn't have been anywhere else on the record, so we just put into The Vault.

<u>Brian's Notes for Drumming:</u> Starts in with a light cadence and then eases into a laid back groove for the verse. In the choruses, the vocals are just accenting straight down beats, so I play a lot of accents on the up beats to syncopate it.

Photographer Unknown

Ultima Esperanza

I was visiting some old punk friends in Germany— Bremen to be exact—in 1999 and there was this guy in their circle of friends who had an acronym for a name. He was 22 or so and desperately in love with a 17-year-old gothic paraplegic girl from Texas he'd met on the internet. They were engaged to be married. They had never met in person. Her name was Ultima Esperanza, which means, I believe, "Last Hope" in Spanish.

I couldn't not write a song about this.

I am really fascinated by how the Internet and the resulting hyper-communication were affecting our hearts. This is sort of the flipside to "Modern Moonlight," which was more of a rant. This one is more of an inside-out love story. I was least happy with the sonic results of this song until I realized, poetically, that it actually sounds best when listened to through bad laptop speakers.

I got to meet Ultima herself about 5 years ago, when she came to see us in Houston. She was indeed beautiful and as sweet as can be.

The wedding was called off.

<u>Brian's Notes for Drumming:</u> I liked the texture of just the quiet, rolling sixteenth notes on the snare in the quiet verses and then building the dynamic over the course of the song. There's a similar effect in the song, "Hyperballad", by Björk that I believe inspired it.

The Gardener

Playing unfamiliar instruments is a good way to write songs. During the same cold Somerville winter that yielded "Modern Moonlight," I was hunting around town for musicians to play with and collided with a bassist/hairdresser named Steven. We made an appointment to try to play together and we made the terrible mistake of picking up a case of beer to make our rehearsal exciting. I think the rehearsal proper only lasted about an hour before the evening disintegrated into an excellent party. He left his bass at my house. I picked it up one day and played three notes.

This is that song. Sometimes songs only need three notes. We played this song live on our last tour and I used a wireless mic and walked around singing in the audience while Brian played drums and bass. It was always really powerful. The last night of tour some really drunk girl grabbed me from behind and felt me up while I was singing this and I couldn't help but notice the poetry of it all.

Brian's Notes for Drumming: This is one that I play either electric bass or acoustic guitar and also work the kick drum and hi-hat pedals on. Not much to say except that you should keep a solid, moody groove on it, or come at it with something of your own invention.

Lonesome Organist Rapes Page-Turner

This was the one of two official B-side releases from Yes, Virginia. Why it's even called a B-side anymore I don't fucking know; people don't buy 45s anymore and they don't really buy CD singles, either. Come to think of it, they don't buy CDs. Chances are if you're reading this, you downloaded our album for free. It's the future! The future is so inspiring.

This was actually a track you could only get on the Japanese version of the album (along with a studio version of "Two-Headed Boy" by Neutral Milk Hotel that weren't very in love with). This song is one of Brian's favorites to play...it's the very punk side of punk cabaret.

I wrote this song when I was about 17—it's the oldest one of the whole collection. I was undergoing a Smiths/Morrissey obsession at the time and I think you can tell.

The reason we recorded this as a B-side was funny in itself. While we were recording at Allaire, Brian remembered this song completely out of the blue. We'd played it a few times in a rehearsal—years before—and he remembered really liking it. I went to pull the lyrics off my computer only to find that the song was so old that I didn't have them on there. So I holed up in my room, tried to remember them, ran back downstairs, practiced it two or three times with Brian and we tracked it within the hour.

We hadn't written an ending, as you can tell from this recording. That's Brian screaming out of sheer primal drummer-ness. And those last three piano notes were our little band in-joke: they're the last three notes that Mozart plays when he disses all over Salieri's welcome march for the emperor in Amadeus (one of our favorite movies of All Time). In rehearsals I often end every song like that. Then Brian does best Tom-Hulce-as-Amadeus obscene giggle. We're fucking dorks.

Brian's Notes for Drumming: This is another peppy one. Lock it in at 220 bpm. Feel free to go all out on the ending as well. The weirdness you hear on the recording is Amanda and I going for totally different endings and the train wreck that ensues. So there is a total, Hail-Mary, joke drum fill that ends in me screaming out of exasperation (and glee). You can hear Amanda capping it off with the final notes as a reference to one of our favorite parts in the film, Amadeus, where Mozart is mocking Saliari by turning a piece of Saliari's music from a modest little tune, into something brilliant and rubs it in his face with the flourish at the end.

Pictured L to R : BRIAN VIGLIONE and AMANDA PALMER

THE DRESDEN DOLLS

Sorry Bunch

I wrote this song for Brian.

In the early days of the band, we were always banging against each other, both physically and emotionally. I kicked him in the balls (by accident!!!) one day. I just called and asked if he would email his side of the story:

"In the summer of 2005, Amanda kicked me, half-accidentally, in the jimmy-jam whilst we were seated opposite each other on a bench seat in the tour van, tooling though Berlin. My face went red, then purple, then green and finally faded to pale grey. It raised my vocal range by three notes and now I can sing 'Delilah.'"

Wise ass.

He, on the other had, rammed into me while we were riding bikes one day and I had to go to the hospital. But he was nice and held my hand while they were stitching my foot up and kept me distracted by promising me that someday our band would be famous and I'd get to wear clothes like Prince in the Purple Rain era. I remember that moment very well.

This song was my way of attempting to say: we're pathetic but at least we're trying. I played it for him the day after I wrote it when we were at some radio session in Boston and I think I might have made him cry.

I can't remember.

Brian's Notes for Drumming: This is one of the first songs Amanda used as a way to get me to start singing live. I was terrified, but I got over it eventually through constant encouragement. Love playing this song now.   This one is all about keeping it simple.

The Kill

The beginning of this song went through many incarnations as I tried to find the perfect combination of words, which included—at one time or another—"anarchist," "Amazon," "antichrist," "asterisk," "ampersand," "acolyte," "atheist," "anorak," "albatross" and my favorite: "alcoholic," which I decided was just too brutally self-loathing so I changed it to "accidental." I later learned that I confused "asterisk" with "asterix." I always assumed they were the same. I fucked up.

This song is, I think, about lying while admitting it, a sort of sonic MC Escher paradox.

The original mix included a coda that lasted an extra minute and a half, but we canned it. It may appear someday on the Internet.

For those of you living overseas and thankfully inured to American pop culture, Pat Sajak was the host of a television game show called Wheel Of Fortune. He and his lovely foam-letter-cube-turning hostess, Vanna White—and all of their fabulous hair—were icons of the 1980s.

Pat Sajak is also a frequent contributor to a newspaper called Human Events. Their slogan is "Leading the Conservative Movement Since 1944." According to their website, they are also the home of "Jihad Watch," the fearless watchdog column that alerts you to the true intentions and deadly plots of the greatest threat to world peace since the fall of the Soviet Union!!!

Someone in the Brigade a while back made some fabulous buttons that read "Put Pat Sajak Back In Office." I still have one and so does Max. He wears it on a plaid vest.

art by Pat Maguire

Brian's Notes for Drumming: The end of this song was especially informed by Dave Grohl's amazing drumming on Nirvana's, In Utero. He was one of my biggest inspirations growing up and I use so much of what I learned from him in my playing to this day.

The Sheep Song

This song is weird.

Sometimes two images collide and stick with you as having to be paired in song form. In this case it was an image of two sheep: one stuffed animal and one on a dinner plate. I have to admit, I think this song may have been inspired—as odd as it seems—by the episode of the Simpsons where Lisa goes Vegetarian. There's a scene in which she looks down at two lambchops and they morph into two adorable little lambs desperately bleating "Liii-iii-iiii-i-iiiisa!!! Don't eee-eee-ee-ee-eeeat us!" It stuck somehow.

Brian's voice was so beautiful on this and our vocals blended so weirdly on the tape that people in the control room thought that he was me and I was him.

Adding the organ on this one was a last minute decision that I think makes this song perfect. It's a heavy-metal lullaby.

Brian's Notes for Drumming: Simply bashes the hell out of the choruses in time with the piano. The verses are in 4/4, the choruses are just a measure 5 and then a measure of 6.

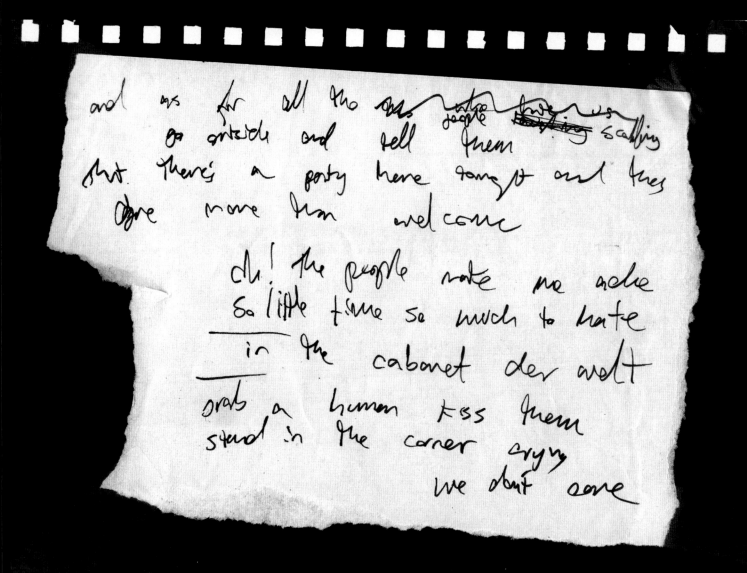

Boston

I remember playing "Boston" for the first time to an audience of one, the night after I wrote it.

He understood, exactly, but things still fell apart.

<u>Brian's Notes for Drumming:</u> Another song I absolutely love to play live. It's made me cry numerous times during shows at the end. I love it.   The verses are played with brushes to add just a subtle pulse, like a ballad. One of my favorite albums with brushes is John Coltrane & Johnny Hartman. Elvin Jones' brushwork is masterful, filled with sensitivity, fluidity, and control and the way he plays behind the beat lends tremendous mood and sensuality to the songs. That's what inspires me to pick up the brushes.

"There is nothing in the world that we can count on.

 Even that we will wake up is an assumption…"
You got that right. So live it like you mean it and play like there's no tomorrow.

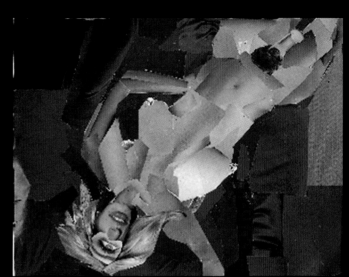

art by Jessica Wright

WWW.DRESDENDOLLS.COM

Photographs by Amanda Palmer
Design by Sarah Gensert, Mark Berger at
Madison House Design

THE DRESDEN DOLLS *Sing*

THE DRESDEN DOLLS *Sing*

SEX
CHANGES

Dear Mis and or Mr ~~sender~~ sender

we're pleased to tell you that your applications been accepted

~~please find enclosed~~ your ~~current~~ ~~species~~ is ~~on~~ gendered

we'll have the details for you after payment is collected

we're due to cut you ~~off~~ today

here is a video called what will all your neighbours say

you cannot own but you can borrow

we'l have the glue to stick the mask on that will stay

on through tomorrow and tomorrow and tomorrow...

~~first we will break you out seeing~~

~~you get an infinitive an aesthetic~~

we have to take your clock out

tick tock tick tock tick tock tick tock

~~we'll get you~~ you the miracle of science fiction

pretty numb but pretty

don't worry we've got you protected

we see it's not what you expected

but you can't ~~fix~~ it once it's ripped off

we're due to ~~cut~~ you up today

~~it's what you the boys go mad for it~~ what will who Nsay

~~and you so sure you want the~~ you lay down full

it ~~might~~ look nice to look at you wake up

today it's don't forget you're stuck with it hollow

SEX CHANGES
C over G ———— add hi → then Downbeats

dear mr and/or mrs sender-
we're pleased to inform you that your applications been accepted
starting from the time you get this letter
your life will be one never-ending "hope you're feeling better"
you get your choice of an aesthetic
we'll need to chop your clock off (tick tock tick tock tick tock tick tock)
it might not be what you expected
but there's no money back once you've been ripped off...

today's a very special day
the boys'll murder for it but what will the neighbors say
it leaves you feeling sort of hollow
it might be nice to look at - don't forget you're stuck with it tomorrow (and tomorrow, and tomorrow....)
intar — — _downbeats_
you're big enough to stop pretending ← BASS
you'll start to really show within a week or so
so don't go saying its just come to your attention
you'll get more than you're asking for without the right protection

today's a very special day
and how you'd love to have a little thing with which to play
but love wont get you very far
today be still your beating heart
youll have to keep on feeding it tomorrow and tomorrow and tomorrow   chorus...
                                        mid

boys will be boys will be boys will be boys will be boys will be boys will beat boys with no warning
girls will be girls will beat guys will beat boys that dont cry over toys that they use to beat girls they
despise by the morning
they always said that sex would change you...

no second thoughts the knife is nearing
you'll never hear the little pitter patter pitter patter
of this little feat of engineering
of course i love you and of course its what inside that matters
but i think this whole charade is ending
it seems to me to be the only way to keep from getting
caught up in a long life of regretting
the doctors said that once you get a taste for it you'll keep on cutting

but while you happen to be here
why dont you whisper all those sweet forevers in my ear
stiff upper lip for all the sorrow
hurry up and stick it in
you never when it will end
tomorrow or tomorrow or tomorrow...
        chorus..... — — — —

        change you → etc

153

Sex Changes

Dear Mis - ter and   or Mrs. - send - er,   we're pleased to in - form you that your

hol - low. ___

It might be nice to look at, don't for - get you're stuck with it to-mor-

- row, and to-mor - row, and to-mor - row... Huh!

You're big e - nough to stop pre-tend - ing.

157

BACKSTABBER

the record goes
from blue to gold
~~right on the right road~~
~~to see~~
you never know
so for a moment
~~please~~ forgive my hyperbole

and penalty inbetwen
there's plenty that you
can't see
you've never known
you'll now get what I mean

you always struck me as the type to take it lightly
but now youre gonna have to shut your mouth or fight me

backstabber…..

your all alone
your all over
the popular magazines
will never care
what do you care
you're so much above that scene

but you got no right to sit there saying I abuse it
when you only sleep with girls who say they like your music

backstabber backstabber backstabber

you who ~~always~~ used to live not breathe it
~~You who used to be breathe it~~

you've got to mean it like you mean it when you mean it when you
say you could've been the only one I could've loved
I want to hear you beg and pray it cause I've never heard you say it
in the way I hear you mean it ~~in the songs~~

Your

even you can't rise above it
~~take~~ your cold embrace and sh…
show

or am I wrong?
nah, I'm never wrong.

so here you go
the open road
is covered with taco stands
and you can stop
we'll drop you off
and write to you when we land

it drives me mad to see your passion when we're fucking
and then you're back to being bored with life by morning
I wish your wild staring eyes that pierce the ceiling to the sky
would keep on going without knowing that you're cumming

Backstabber

MODERN
MOONLIGHT

presenting modern moonlight just as advertised
coke and pepsi finally hit a compromise
how can they complain that we're all fucked up kids
when they keep on changing who our mother is

but to be completely honest
night is in the way of progress

wire cutters of the world
you know what to use it for
spread the word to all the tightrope walker boys and girls

retinas are bleeding for the enterprise
surgically wired into paradise
yesterday I went to mattie's funeral
everyone was messaging like it was going out of style
it was just the cynic in me
god I love communicating
I just hate the shit I'm missing

everybody join in the magnificence
everything is absolutely making sense
every single man and woman, girl and boy
a rousing chorus of "the spangled and the beautiful
the mangled un-unconnectable the speed of just survival
and the one who dies the fastest takes it all"

inst

fight it all you want it's useless
life is in the way of progress

wire cutters of the world
rise and make your scissors heard
cut with an abanndon you have never known before
brace yourself america
youre in for a nasty shock
when the war is over you can read the paper

Modern Moonlight

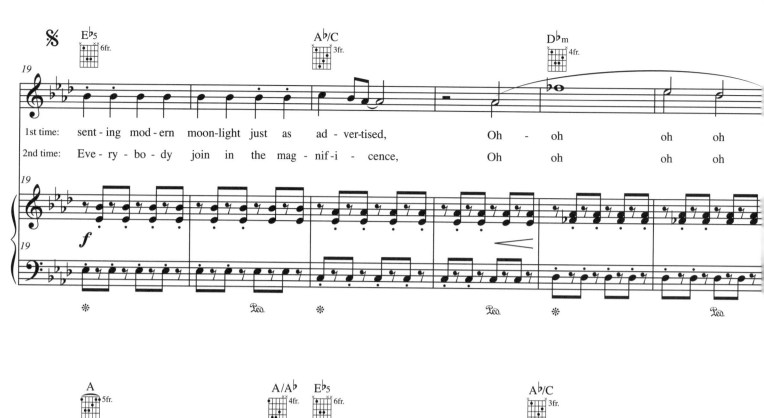

1st time: sent - ing mod - ern moon-light just as ad - ver-tised, Oh - oh oh oh
2nd time: Eve - ry - bo - dy join in the mag - nif - i - cence, Oh oh oh oh

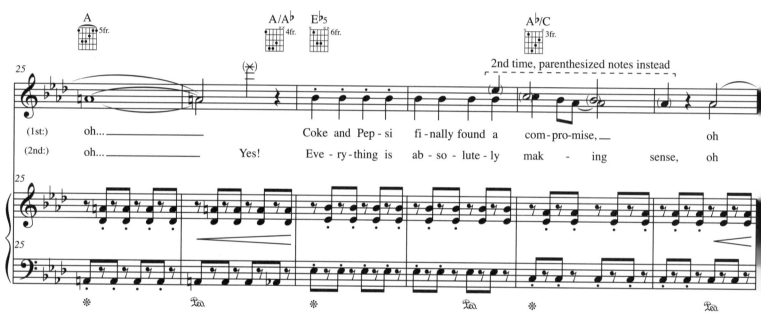

2nd time, parenthesized notes instead

(1st:) oh... Coke and Pep - si fi - nally found a com-pro-mise, oh
(2nd:) oh... Yes! Eve - ry-thing is ab - so - lute - ly mak - ing sense, oh

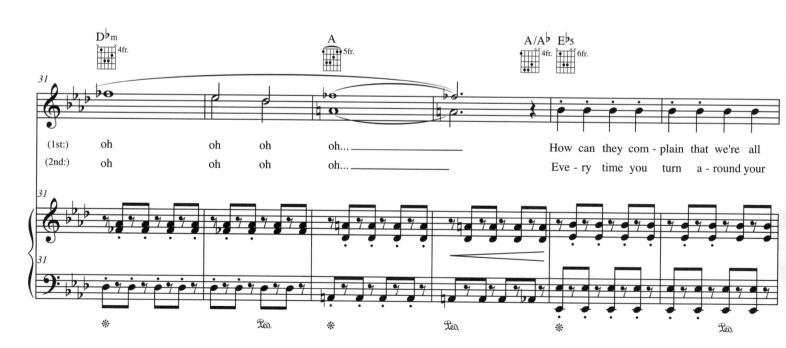

(1st:) oh oh oh oh... How can they com - plain that we're all
(2nd:) oh oh oh oh... Eve - ry time you turn a - round your

Like it all you want, it's fruit-less.

Night is in the way of prog-ress.

1st time: Ret-i-nas are bleed-ing for the en-ter-prise, oh

2nd time: Yes-ter-day I dropped in at the M - K - B, oh

2nd time, parenthesized notes instead

180

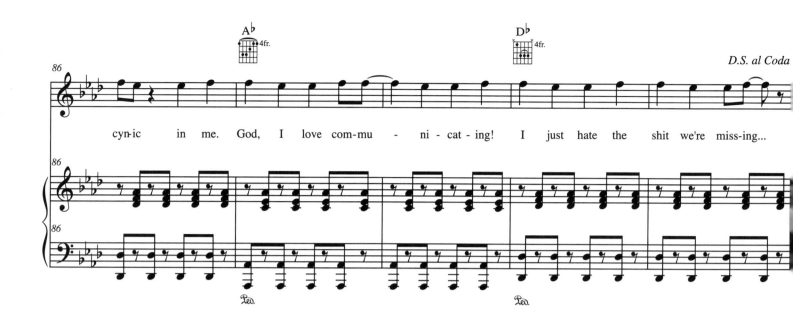

cyn-ic in me. God, I love com-mu - ni - cat - ing! I just hate the shit we're miss-ing...

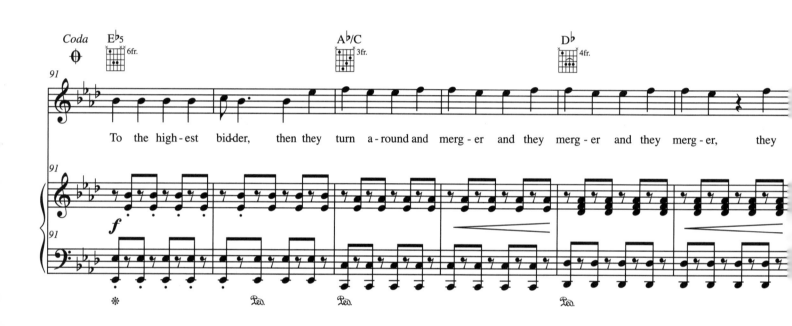

To the high-est bid-der, then they turn a - round and merg - er and they merg - er and they merg - er, they

(Guitar - arpeggiate (if crazy) or strum)

mur - der, and they mur - der. The one who mur-ders most will take it all...

MY ALCOHOLIC FRIENDS

(A) I'm counting back
the number of the steps
it took for me to get
back on the wagon for the weekend

$E^b A B E^b$

I'm actually small
the light is casting out
the shadow in the hall
where I appear to be exploding

(B) I'll use the autotimer to prove that I
got home with my imagination
when they find the body in the basement
"in the very house that she was raised in!"

cresc. fall

(A) I'm marking down
the number of the Times
so when we get the sign
from god I'll be the first to call them

(B) I'm taking back the number of the beast
cause 6 is not a pretty number
8 or 3 are definitely better
a is for the address on the letters to

"Alc" my alcoholic friends $E/A/E/A$

(B-top) all the way from Brooklyn to Boston
if i live through this infatuation
will I turn into a ticking time bomb
set to blow before they bring the breadsticks

(C) I'll be on my best behavior
taking shots for mother nature
once my fist is in the cupboard
love is never falling

I'm.......

(B) I'm trying hard
not to be ashamed
not to know the name
of who is waking up beside me
or the date, the season or the city
but at least the ceilings very pretty
and if you are holding it against me

v2.

(C) I'll be on my best behavior
taking shots for mother nature
once my fist is in the cupboard
love is never falling over

(B-top) should I choose a noble occupation
if I did I'd only show up late and
sick and they would stare at me with hatred
plus my only natural talent's wasted on

I'm counting back the number of the steps
it took for me to get ~~back in~~
~~the wagon~~ back in the wagon of the weekend
~~never~~ never my ~~staying~~
and I'm ~~writing~~ down the license of your car
before you got to far so I can ~~park~~ in the ~~parking~~
prove it station
I got home with my imagination
if they find my body in the basement
I'll be in my ~~head~~ believing
taking shots for mother nature
once my head is in the cupboard
love is ~~falling~~ falling over

~~I'm finding out the letters in a word~~
~~are never seen or heard without the~~
I'm taking back the promise that I made
In my innocent state we know what
I'm ~~writing~~ down the number of the times
So when we get a sign
from god I'll be the first to tell
I'm counting off the objects in the room then

My Alcoholic Friends

in the cup-board love is nev-er fall-ing o-ver.

Huh!

One, two, three, four! Should I choose a

no-ble oc-cu-pa-tion? If I did, I'd on-ly show up late and sick and they would

DELILAH

 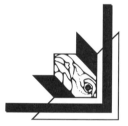

art by Amanda Palmer

Delilah

196

205

Let's see___ how___ fast___ this___ thing___ can go...___ oh_____ oh...___

...oh___ oh_____ oh___ oh...___

Let's see___ how___ fast___ this___ thing___ can go...___ oh_____ oh...___

...oh___ oh_____ oh___ oh...___

Oh_____ oh_____ oh___ oh...___

mf

DIRTY BUSINESS

raise your ~~bets~~ glass
we have incorporated
~~make your kids~~ place your bets
your coronation   waiting pretty. anticipated
howd you do
on that insignly function
92
its knotted county ~~~~   me

~~to~~ all the ones that hoped ~~~~ the most
a toast ~~becomes them~~ ~~~~ cause it becomes
they ~~~~ all ~~~~   to ~~all the~~   you
~~~~ all the fun ~~~~ to blood ~~and~~ ~~~~
any other day I'd ~~~~ ~~~~ throat to reconcile
~~~~   ~~~~ ~~~~ champagne
                        on ~~~~ triumphant smile
I'll ~~have~~   your (you're getting closer)
you stole ~~~~ from your watching
me and my ~~committee~~ have decided
        ~~regrets will~~ ~~~~ ~~~~ you down
        ~~~~ that you've ~~~~ worth stopping
        ~~~~ ~~~~   won the ~~first~~ toaster

take a bow and take the trophy ~~~~
~~~~ ~~~~ ~~~~ ~~~~ ~~~~
        ~~~~ ~~~~ ~~~~ like me
know how much your insults mean to me
and my committee have decided
your the best we've seen ~~~~
                        since J Matt Pepe

to all the girls of pearl
to all the ~~~~ ~~a~~   for each and every one
~~~~ so I've ~~a~~ prizes ~~~~
                        but please be patient

she's the kind of girl who looks for silver linings in a dumpster ~~truck~~
she's the girl ~~who promises the world to you if you~~ gets you she's ~~its~~ bipolar ~~it make you~~ ~~trust me~~
she's the kinds of girl who leaves out condoms on her bedside dresser
just to make you jealous of the men she ~~fucked~~ ~~had~~ before you met her

to all the ones who thought they knew me ~~best~~ last
a test to prove your ~~prowess~~ ~~first and~~
who was mine in 99 I want names and
~~full~~ ~~addresses~~ current status ~~last~~ full

to all the ones.
           ~~dirty business~~

        poster girl for rotten first impressions
          ~~imagine~~ bad decisions
          hope ~~hope~~ ~~dreams~~ t
  now its up   to you   from   what to do
                 it's pretty dirty business

call my bluff

Dirty Business

210

(1st:) She's the kind of girl who on-ly asks you o-ver when its rain-ing, just to make you lie there catch-ing wa-ter drip-ping from the ceil-ing.

(2nd:) She's the kind of girl who leaves out con-doms on the bed-room dress-er just to make you jeal-ous of the men she fucked be-fore you met her.

Lift your hats off to the check-out girls with tat-tooed backs. They'd make an an - gel's skin crawl.

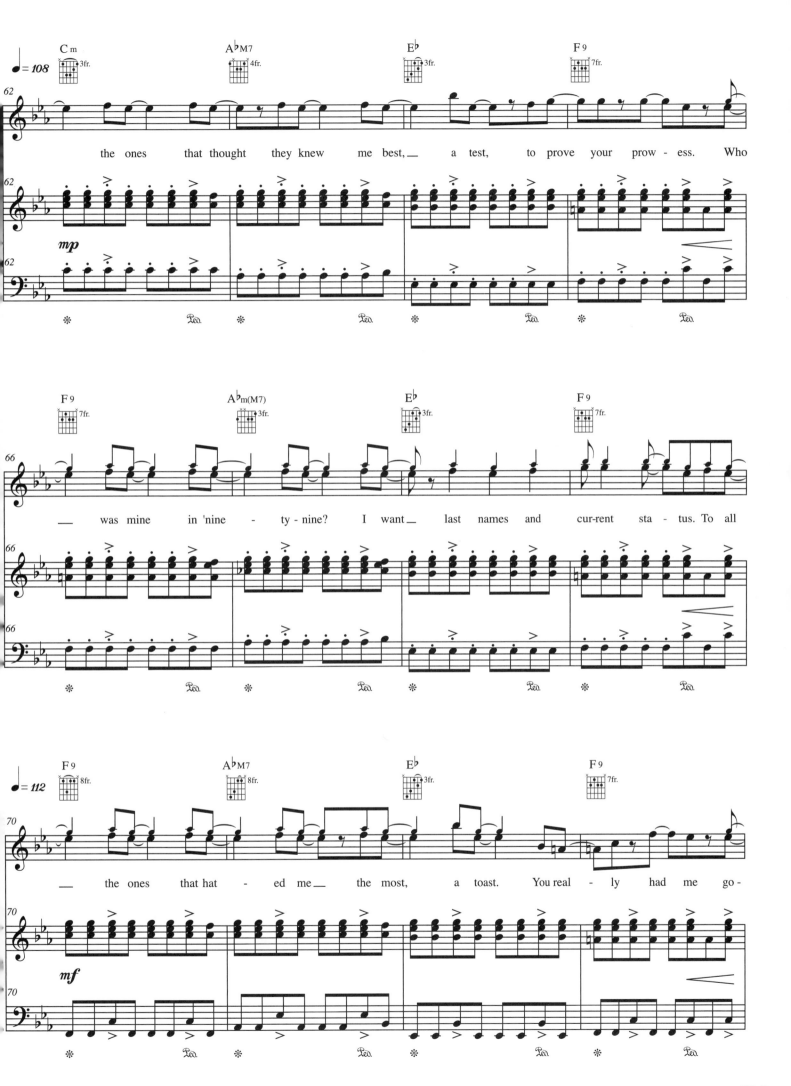

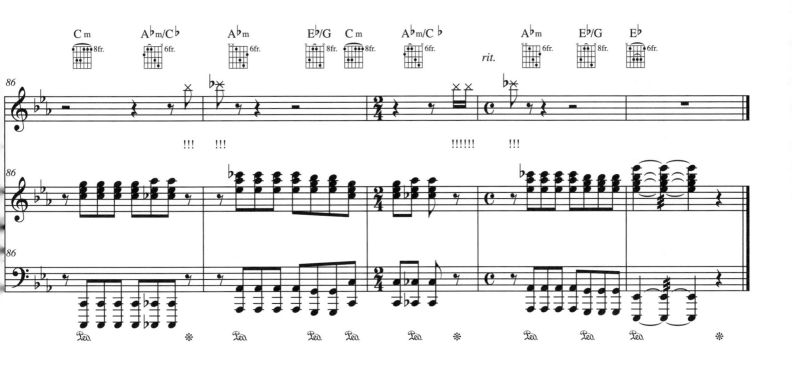

FIRST ORGASM

THE FIRST ORGASM OF THE MORNING
A

it is a thursday
I get up early
it's quite a challenge
i'm kind of lazy *because i'm lazy* *i'm usually lazy* *would last notes.*

i make some coffee
I eat some rice chex
and then i sit down
to check my inbox

i only read a word or two
i stare across the street and see the churches and the blue

the first orgasm of the morning
is hard and raw as hell
there wont be any second coming
as far as i can tell

i arch my back cause
i'm very close now
it's very cold here
by the window

there are some school kids
yelling and running
i barely notice
that i am cumming

the first orgasm of the morning
is like a fire drill
nice to have a little warning
but not enjoyable

i am too busy to have friends
a lover would just complicate my plans
i will never look for love again
i'm taking matters into my own hands

i think i could last at least a week without someone to hold me
i think i could last at least a week without someone to hold me
won't you hold me?

ADF#
G#
ADF#
G#
ADA
and
Dmaj7

219

First Orgasm

220

MRS. O

o mrs o

will you tell us where the naughty children go
will you show
how the sky turned white and everybody froze
heaven knows how they got into the fireplace
but everybody's saying grace
and trying to keep a happy face

and o mrs o
can you teach us how to keep from getting cold
off we go and you watch us as we face the falling snow
what a show with our hairdryers aimed heavenwards
and fifty foot extension cords
you really have a way with words

the truth cant save ~~you~~ us now
the sky is falling down
~~in the dark it may look scary~~
~~but its very quite contrary~~

oh mrs o ~~tell us~~ the one about ~~alssm~~
tell us rosy stories when the ashes blow
what you chose to leave out of it is chilling to the bone
we all know
there's no hell and no hiroshima
chernobyl was a cover-up the world is really all in love

and o mrs o
will you tell about the time they made you go
~~lined in rows~~ to the palace where they took your only clothes
we all know
theres no hitler and no holocaust no winter and no santa claus
and yes virginia all because
the truth cant save you now
the sky is falling down
~~and we can't stop the mobs from lying~~
~~but like children we keep trying~~
~~everything within our power~~
~~april trains may bring strange showers~~

oh mrs o
will you leave us hanging now that we are grown
up and old
will you kill me if i say i told you so
we all know
there's no heaven and no ~~consequence~~
the rest is anybody's guess
but yes virginia you can trust us there will be a place for us
the truth cant save you now
the sky is falling down
eveything they ever told us
~~breaks our faith they broke their~~ promise
but you can stop the truth from leaking
if you never stop believing......

[handwritten annotations in margins, partially legible:]
& watch the vultures cont. the hours
april trains may bring strange showers
the world is really all in love
all love
hitler and hiroshima
chernobyl was a cover up
every tale a twist shakes our faith
and breaks their promise

6

Mrs. O

say - ing grace and try-ing to keep a hap - py face. And real - ly have a way with words. The truth won't
ten - sion cords. You

save ___ you ___ now, ah ah oh... The sky is fall - ing down, ah ah oh...

___ Watch the vul - tures count the hours. ___ A - pril

SHORES of CALIFORNIA

he's been trying with limited success
to get this girl to let him get into her pants
but every time he thinks he's getting close
she threatens death before he gets a chance

that's the way it is in minnesota
and that's the way it is in Oklahoma homa
that's the way it's been since protozoa
first crawled on the shores of California

and she's been trying with limited success
to get him to turn off the lights and dance
cause like any girl she just wants
that fickle little bitch romance   x2

its strangles every relationship
they argue and they try to navigate
and if she loves him she'll put up with it
but if she don't they'll probably gonna split

that's the way it is in arizona
and that's the way it is in Oklahoma homa
that's the way since the animal and noah
washed up on on the shores of California

and that is why a guy is called a sleaze
and that is why a girl is called a tease
and that's why god made escort agencies
one life to live and dynasty   x2

he says I'm completely full of shit
he says most girls are secretly begging for it
but I think he's just pussywhipped
and every story goes like this

so say what you want the cause is
insignificant it doesn't matter who is wrong or right
my friends not getting laid tonight
that's the way it is in nova scotia
and that's the way it is in Oklahoma homa
the way since Aristophanes and homer
wrote the iliad and lysistrata

why do we have conflicting specifications
maybe to prevent overpopulation
all I know is that all around the nation
girls are cryin' and boys are masturbatin'
girls are dancin' and the boys are all just waiting   x2

so say what you want the cause is
insignificant it doesn't matter who is wrong or right
my friends not getting laid tonight
that's the way it is in minnesota
and that's the way it is in Oklahoma homa
that's the way it's been since protozoa
first crawled on the shores of California

[handwritten annotations:]
F love
F thing
F
F
Ab
F thing
F
but we aint far
what's it matter tonight if he's right
must not feel too kind
stop thinking love is blind
clench my fists + write
he's just not my type
(F) section .5
F
x2
CAPS

233

Shores of California

234

239

NECESSARY EVIL

ines get crossed
signals lost
it is an ordinary evening yeah
I am broadcasting are you receiving yeah?
I remember golden days when all this was a luxury and
~~backend~~ it doesn't ~~first~~ ~~mea~~ when ~~you~~ ~~turn~~ the screen on me
~~matter~~ when you go erasing me
and ~~the cards~~ ~~days~~ go by
~~digits/values~~ Fly
~~It is an ordinary evening~~ it is a measurable feeling
7 on a scale from ~~good~~ to grieving

~~that star~~
~~different~~ ~~bands~~ ~~lines are down~~ innocence ~~infuriates~~ me
~~the golden sands~~ all fall down your ~~selection~~
~~different~~ ~~sands~~ ~~there is an emptiness~~ ~~that~~ ~~going~~ ~~me~~
~~it is~~ a ~~unsettling~~ wondering if you should SKIP
every ~~single~~ ~~time~~ that you erase me or save me
send a simple message and you'll save me

The connected ~~voices~~ wires to my ~~letters~~ ~~editors~~ in the ~~discotheques~~
they don't know the difference ~~because~~ ~~honestly~~ is it live ~~why~~ ~~is~~ ~~it~~ ~~recorded~~ ~~girl~~
and if you find yourself without me (X3) ~~memorex~~
then ~~not only~~ (can you?) then is ~~unless~~ I'll ~~come~~ ~~for~~ ~~you~~
don't be too alarmed I've gone from speech to text!

next in line
bonafide
it is a necessary evil
~~better~~ ~~puppet~~ ~~images~~ ~~than~~ ~~people~~
~~better~~ ~~than~~ ~~them~~ ~~us~~
~~too many~~ there's ~~you~~ ~~get~~ in line to ~~fish~~ in the genepool.

A
scarves get lost fingers crossed
it is an ordinary evening
i am broadcasting are you recieving

eight foot pound all fall down
your lack of tact infuriates me
wondering if you should skip or save me

i remember golden days when all this was a luxury
but i pretend it doesnt matter when you go outdating me
and if you find yourself without me
if you find yourself without me
can you find yourself without me
then and only then when i'll
come for you

mark set go
who is refereeing what we're even fucking playing i don't know
it is a measurable feeling
seven on a scale from dead to breathing
i've connected speakers to my suitors at the discotheques
and they dont know the difference:
is it live, or is it memorex?
and if you find yourself without me
if you find yourself without me
can you find yourself without me
then and only then is when i'll
come for you

-key change-

i remember golden days when all this was a mystery
and you could write a letter then or god forbid come visit me
and if you find yourself without me
and if you find yourself without me and
if you find yourself without me
if you find yourself without me
can't you find yourself without me?
if you find yourself without me
(if you find.........)
if you find yourself without me
if you find yourself without me
then and only then is when i'll
come for you.

244

Necessary Evil

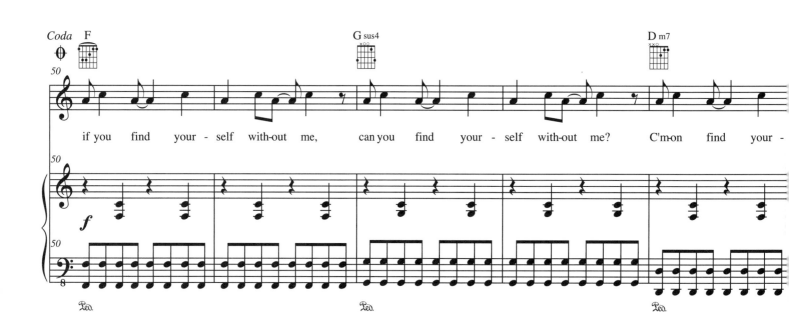

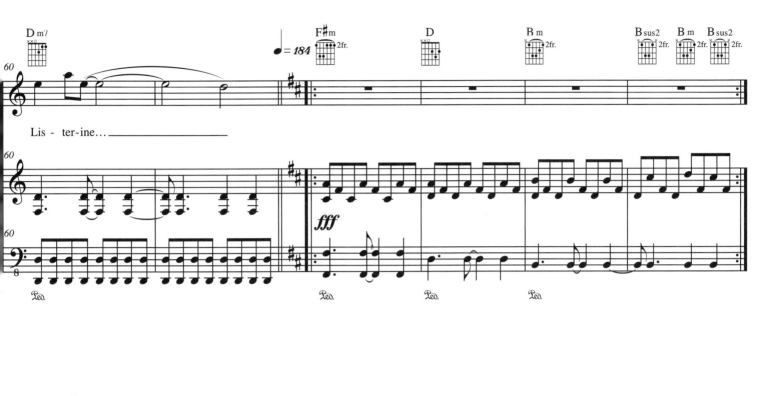

Lis - ter-ine… _____

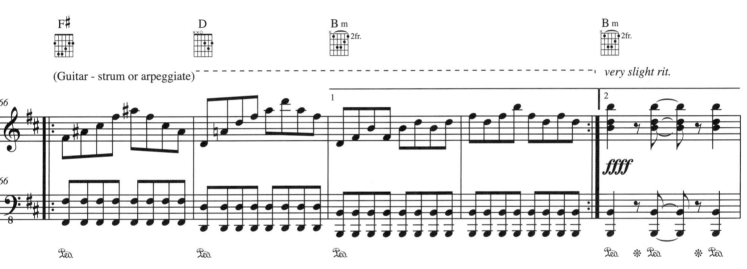

(Guitar - strum or arpeggiate) - very slight rit.

I re-mem - ber gold-en days when all this was a mys - ter - y. ___And

(Right Hand *8va* 2nd time)

you could write a let-ter then, or God for-bid, come vis-it me. vis-it me. And

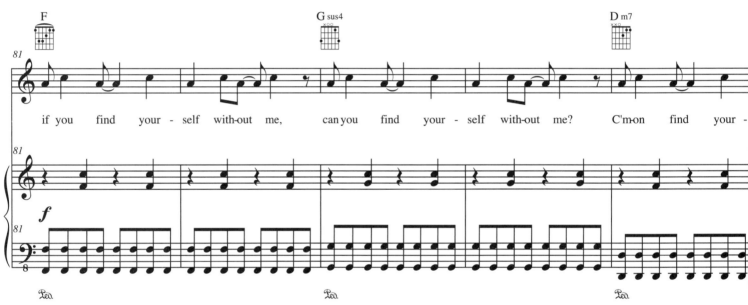

if you find your-self with-out me, can you find your-self with-out me? C'm-on find your-

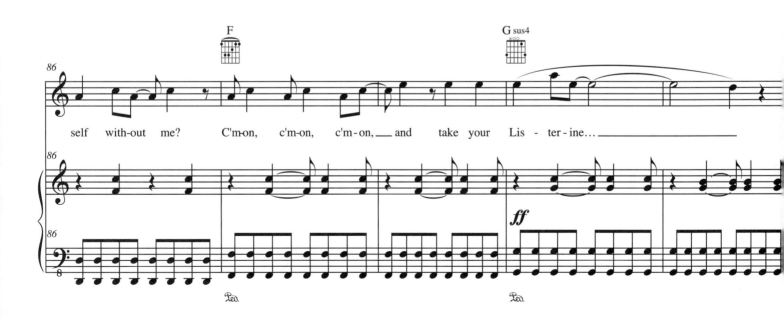

self with-out me? C'm-on, c'm-on, c'm-on, and take your Lis-ter-ine...

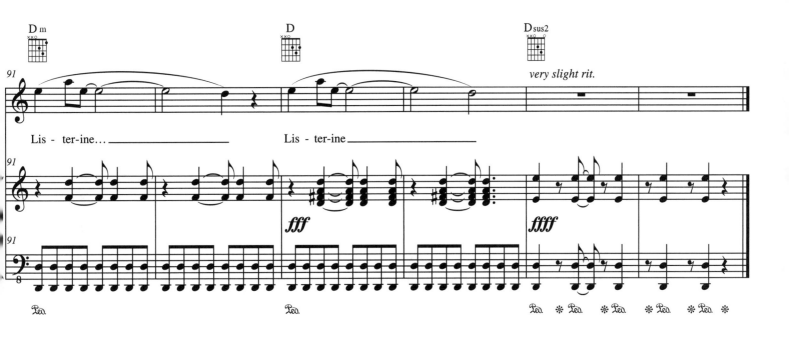

Lis - ter-ine… _____   Lis - ter-ine _____

Mandy Goes to Med School

i've been pulling pricks on the camera
I've been looking slick in a black limo

I've been making eyes
I've been ~~taking~~ ~~tips~~ tips from the taliban
I've been making trips to the bathroom
I've ~~been~~ ~~making~~ ~~selling~~ winding down to the finalists
I've been finding good ways of hiding it
yes I'll tell you everything if you can
give me one good reason

yes I'll bide my time ~~my~~ and I'll strike when I am
~~good~~ ~~and~~ ~~ready~~ ~~made~~ ~~out~~ ~~is~~ ~~my~~
wars made a man of me

yes I'll let you anything that I can guess what you
are ~~thinking~~ bless your soul ~~bless~~ you're headed for
a starring role in this weeks massacre
I've been trading water ~~money~~ for oxygen
I've been getting back to the simple things
I've been ~~saving~~ ~~love~~ ~~for~~ far a nice day
I've been ~~selling~~ ~~good~~ ~~at~~ ~~the~~ ~~home~~ ~~game~~

I've been boiling ekes for the enemy
I've been making meat from the gravy
I've been finding ghosts in the alleyway
stained and sussed and nearly foot Hollywood

dead from the waist down
dumb from the neck up
drowned out and washed out
pinned down + stuck up
dead from the waist down
washed out and jacked-up
I'm heading downtown
ready for the final cut

yes I'll give you everything I have
to lose ~~this~~ this flimsy g-string
tune me to your key and ~~and~~ and baby
I'll agree to just about anything

READY FOR
THE FINAL CUT.

254

yes i'll get just the thing you need to be the next best thing
lets start in with ~~the simple~~ test ~~and in no time we'll get you running~~

a ask my *~~of~~ your intelligence and sense of timing*

guess how many fingers in ~~ma~~ guess how many things ~~i put there~~ can fit there *more i can fit them*
guess right get the toaster but you know sir guessing gets you nowhere

sundays
one way to deal ~~w~~ it
(might of it)

i've been ~~baking cakes~~ for the enemy *making eyes at*
i've been trying to find out the hard way
~~i've been buying stock in the alleyways~~ *the lion dining, bets on the runaways*
~~index upwards onwards and anyway~~ ~~some ones dance~~ *no one's matched my ante but my way*

yes i bet you anything that i can guess what you are thinking
crackpot schemeing crackhead ~~spinning~~ *~~dreaming~~* crazy but arent you still listening

kiss your woes goodbye say hi to bliss ~~and pose with your slice of the~~ *tens on the backsides of your*
~~pie times any number piek your poison toss it in the blender~~ *like a wish for* *~~long~~* *Alyson and*

i've been ~~making shakes~~ for the ~~taliban~~ *making eyes shakes contraband* *now put down the gun + kiss your* *so sister*
making frequent trips to the bathroom
~~jumping on the wagon and riding it~~ *prove me wrong but*
got i've been ~~finding good ways~~ of hiding it *~~trips my~~ theres no denying it*

i;ve been making eyes at the bad guys
i've making up for lost time
enemy
wars made a man of me

yes i'll tell you just the thing you need to do the next best thing
get one part love to two parts war and add a dash of nitro-glycerin

i've been getting up-close and intimate
some close calls but i'm getting into it
in some towns they say you can burn for it
but ill burn that bridge when i get to it

so what say we take a spin ~~i'll bring you up to speed and~~ *im my* ~~brand spanking new~~ *hospital gown landry bin*

~~im not a bad boy~~ *It's not a bad thing*
~~it's super cool~~ *supercool*
it's got a nice ring:
Mandy goes to ~~med school~~ med school

sit down + take my medicine

Mandy Goes to Med School

but I'll burn that bridge when I get to it.

It's not a bad thing to get pro-fes-sion-al.

It's got a nice ring.

261

Oh, Man - dy goes to med school,

oh _____ la ___ la ___ ah ah... Huh!

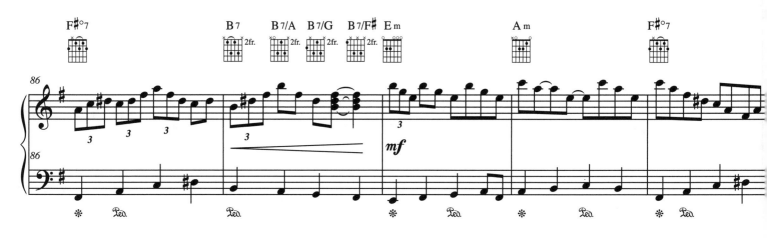

ME
and the
MINIBAR

bring two prix fixe dinners up
I'll unwrap the plastic cups
it's just us my love
it's just us my love

I will clean the room up nice
put your insides all on ice
it was real true love
it was real true love

close all the windows
put signs on the handles
and strip down to my dun-dun-duns
you have gone too far
you have gone so far

and tonight — to dim
its just me and the minibar (just up to diminished)

candles from the walmart that
every city to have
that I bought last night
that I bought last night

I was so excited to
do such normal things with you
when you left last night
with your toothbrush dry

no such details will spoil my plan
that is the kind of girl I am   ha ha ha
                                    dundundundun

change melody
from 1st O

can you hear room 818?
man they're really happening
they're a wild bunch
they're a wild bunch

but if they just knew
what my night was coming too
god would they vomit and run
you have gone too far
you have gone too far
and tonight
it's just me and the minibar
nobody else
and I sing at the top of my lungs
happy birthday us
happy birthday us

Me & The Minibar

268

its just me and the min - i - bar.

Can - dles from the Wal - mart that ... eve - ry cit - y's got to have,

that I bought last night, that I bought last night.

SING

there is this thing that's like fucking except you don't fuck
everyone hears it and gets it but no one gets off
all the worlds history's gradually dying from shock
there is this thing that's like talking except you don't talk.......you sing
sing

Bb

sing for the bartender sing for the janitor sing
sing for the president sing for the anarchists sing
sing for the teachers who told you that you couldn't sing
sing cause you never learned how but now who gives a shit
just sing

there is this thing keeping everyone's lungs and lips locked
it is called fear and it's seeing a big renaissance
after the show you can go die wherever you want
but right now let's all pretend we're about to get bombed together!
right now!
just sing
ah – ah –ah

sing like oasis + blur aan forget forget

sing for the emo/metal-kids sing for the audience *arsenlot* sing
sing for the subway the sick and recovering sing
sing for the cameras sing for the teens and sing
sing for kid in the hat who refuses to sing
sing for the teachers who...
take off your sunglasses take off your walkman and sing
take off your eyeliner take off your t-shirt and sing
sing for the laund-e-ry sing for your enemies sing
sing for the baseball team sing for the janjaweed sing

walkman.   *sports bra*

aaaaaaaaaaaahhhhhhhhhhhhhhhhhhhahahahah

cause you've already broken it
cause you're already broke again
cause youre gonna get paid again
cause you're gonna lose everythihng

Bmi: E Eb
A Eb D
sing like oasis + blur con forget + forgive

F#: life is no cabaret
D: we don't care what you say
F: we're inviting you anyway
D: motherfuckers you'll sing someday
you motherfuckers you'll sing someday

we are appalled by a world that is dying of shoc[
I can't do anything you can't do anything but
there is this thing that's like talking except you
you sing
sing
sing

Sing

DEAR JENNY

~~girls~~ boys wear overcoats in heat like this to keep themselves from ~~streaming~~ showing E^{2b}

girls pretend to notice when the sun gees out the scene is every ~~fucking~~

mothers all call doctors all ~~red falling~~ ~~looking~~ for ~~the~~ a certain ~~uses~~ kisses
~~call fucking row of fucking~~

fathers ~~all~~ an aggrivated diet of viagra kisses

~~sad but~~ true $^{top}F\#$ $\rangle C\# E\cdots$ the facts of life are bound to get you down

but look around dear Jenny Anyway the world s

pretty upside down

the raves are better in the   summer...

1st

     C D E♭ B

     E♭ F G♭

     D E♭ B

soldiers wander young ~~forwards~~ donning patriotic colors

who could fight in heat like this and after ~~all~~ they're our brothers

weary o-so-drearily we wave our flags into the camera

bleary-eyed and teary it gets cut up looking tiresome

sad but true the forces of the earth can get you down

but look around dear Jenny anyway...

Mrs ~~Miggins~~ Oaks is whistling above choking on her gin and tonic

                    secret agent alcoholics

sad but true the pistols fire off into the ground

Jenny days my Jenny days my Jenny days my Jenny days my days are
numbered
will soon be over

anyway I cut it will take many lifetimes to
anyway you take it recover
cut it anybody's days till death are
numbered

Jenny plays in space
invaders stares on
whats the true crusaders
Jenny places first in
every contest where
you run for cover
gravity comes sneaking up
comes creeping in
when she is

Jenny days my Jenny days my
Jenny days have come went
in Jenny vs. gravity the court
has ruled she's innocent
as charged

GRAVITY believe me THROWS ME OFF and tugs me HANGING by a single GOLDEN thread when me
JENNY winks BEHIND me PLEASE DONT MOVE! he'll find me! CHOOSING sides NOT Simple tug γ near, INSIDE ME

Jenny plays in fields & daisy chains PINK poppies grazing aves
GRAV. comes CREEPING from behind and QUICK her face is covered
I CRIES and FLIES into the clouds GRIPPED by a sudden FEVER
GRAVITY comes crashing down you atmosphere in TIME to SEIZE her
SAD but TRUE the forces of the world never betray S bound
but THROUGH the miracle of science we can find a way to GET around
CRIPPLED girl the PHYSICS of the world might get you DOWN but look
AROUND dear Jenny anyway the world (is) Onetty upside-down

GRAV. Yet If of me In FACING it numbered I want to break free the toward
I can see my Jenny plays ever if I could write century
GRAV for a go I want to breathe IMPOSSIBLE LOVERS before I myself record
ANYWAY my Jenny Days over
JENNY flies a KITE the BRIGHT SUN BLINDING and until it TANGLES
GRAVITY laughs SADLEDLY as Jenny falls into the BRAMBLES
JENNY gets her COURAGE back and somersaults deep into winter
JENNY 9ts low awhile and plants a FALLING tree + TRICK leaf
GRAVITY lays low awhile

Dear Jenny

Boys wear o- ver-coats in heat like this to keep them-selves from show-ing, girls fill out pre-scrip-tions for the tricks

— that keep their hearts from grow-ing. Spe - cial - ists re-view the year in tears and call for dras - tic meas-ures,

send them to re-sorts for boys and girls to get their wits to - geth-er,

(Together:) Sad but true, the facts of life are bound

293

NIGHT RECONNASSAINCE

Night Reconnaissance

296

one plays a po-et who starts___ up a band of his

own,___ one plays a vol-ley-ball play___-er with both her wrists

broke.

1st time: And we hide_____ from the guns on our night re-con-nais-sance,

2nd time: _____ them good homes, give them love they've nev-er known

Straight 8ths, no swing

(Right hand *8va* 2nd time)

The MOUSE and the MODEL

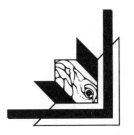

The ___ of the model ~~are~~ ___ ___ ___
___   for someone to trust
they'll ___ it they're desperate →

nothing is certain at this time of day
you could reverberate you could decay
~~the difference it makes is so laughably small~~
~~the time's up the lights up the hole's in the wall~~

The ___ plays ___ on your ___   are awfully
one slip of the   dressa
while nobody's watching
the wrist flicks the tongue slips
you're in for it now

? { let's start a new heart
  { ~~a new sort of stake~~ the new parts don't break
  { we'll take them we'll mate them
  { we'll make them relate

by counting your blessings you fall into in debt
it starts with your family and camps in your bed
and jekyll and hyded when you could have let
your guard down your dress up you must be upset

let's try a new kind of
valentine cheer
we'll shake them we'll break them
and make them sincere

it's dark over here on the flip side of ~~treason~~ reason
the reason ~~could~~ be something easy like
~~i saw it in a book?~~ i didn't even look"?
you're a crook you're a fake you're a dater
if you did it say you did it if you didn't
suck it up and say you did
--- -- - --- -- -

~~let's play a new game~~ let's start a new heart i'm harder than god
~~i'm waiting for god~~ the new parts are ___
we'll tax them relax them
~~and drag them to prom~~ and ask them to prom

{ the vote by a landslide
{ for jekyll and hyde   ✓
{ mackenzie macavity
{ bonnie and clyde

two faced

The Mouse and the Model

307

book." You're a crook, you're a fake, you're com-mit-ted. If you did it, say you did it, if you did-n't, suck it up and say you

did. Ah ah oh... Ah ah oh...

313

ULTIMA ESPERANZA

downloady dubs on his fancy computer
hes shooting for hope in the dark
hey ~~buddy~~ you've found her now go ~~habit~~ message her
name is a pretty good start

ultima ~~sits~~ in her bedroom in texas
and daydreams about being touched
she lost her legs in an ~~accident~~ car crash two years ago ~~from being~~
~~she~~ ~~lonely~~ ~~friend~~ and ~~lovely~~   she doesn't get around much
~~and~~ she is hoping to ~~find~~
someone to know her online
now that you have her ^address you can send her
the ~~pictures~~ you ~~scanned~~   your ~~stairs~~ a matching container for pants
slick rhododendrons you made out of paper
there's no better way to her heart
(don't blow it all ~~at~~ ~~one the time~~) at one time
save ~~something for good for the end~~ dare cross the ~~black~~ dotted line

~~program~~ data streams ~~ooo~~ between bremen and ~~houston~~ austin
she's sending ~~attachments~~ of love
~~opening~~ showing her heart but you don't love the version
~~effort~~ alice to open them up

600 deershments to fix your connection
good love is expensive these days
~~for~~ ~~that~~ much ~~now~~ ~~you could be~~ flying to ~~houston~~ texas
but think of the time that you'll save

what better love than the kind
that ~~stops~~ stirs when your servers offline

Ultima Esperanza

1st time: Down - load - ing doves on __ your fan - cy __ com - put - er, __ you're
2nd time: Now that you got her a dress you can send her a

(1st:) shoot - ing __ for love in __ the __ dark. __
(2nd:) match - ing at - tach - ment and __ face. __

The GARDENER

The hyacinths have blossomed
a colorful display
~~so~~ ~~sharpen~~ your wrists & cross them   / change
we'll let you out today

you are the seed we ~~planted~~
~~but~~ ~~I am~~ ~~sad to say~~   bother -
you're ~~not~~ quite what we wanted
and ~~no-one wants to trade...~~

O is ~~my little~~ (will) ~~and~~ (willow) weeping (weeping)?
drop down to your knees
The untitled skin before me   keep
O! the possibilities!

~~we'll~~ make a man out of you yet!
~~we'll~~ ~~cook you~~ ~~for~~   perfect fit we will plow trenches in your bed
just close your eyes and count to 10   your bed
~~YLB~~ is as close as ~~you~~ ~~will~~ could get

~~plant you~~ ~~among the best~~ ~~later~~
a child is like a ~~nasty little~~ weed you plague me / like a weed
the more ~~you~~ pave him over   begotten
the more ~~they~~ wants to breathe

thank you for the warning
but I still ~~see~~ the sun
a little global warming
never hurt no-one   — is our
do you want another
should I call the nurse?
o no— I beg you ~~father~~

I didn't want the first

The Gardener

327

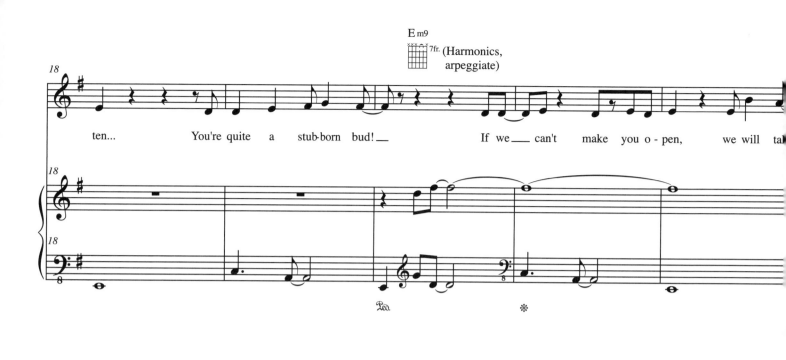

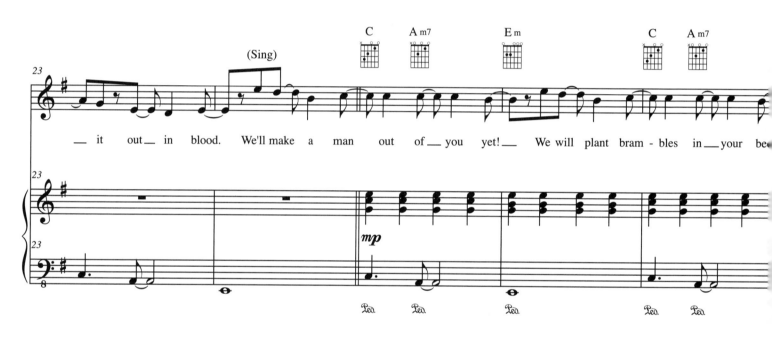

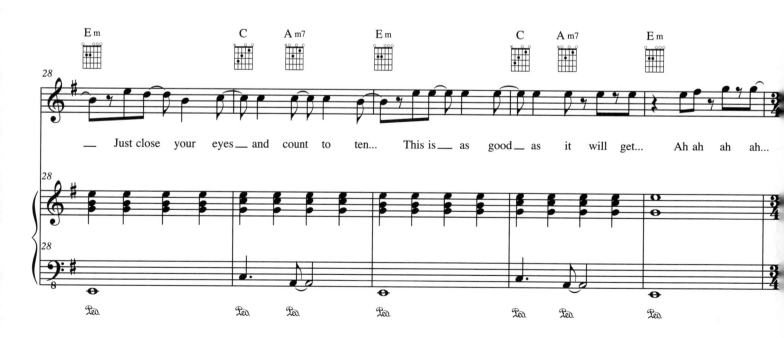

LONESOME ORGANIST RAPES PAGE TURNER

this is as far as I could get.   Fmin →
he jabbed a needle in my head   B♭maj
erasing any evidence
but there were stains ~~on~~ inside my pants
and if a rock should hit my head
and I remember what he did
you'll be the very first to know
maybe I'll find out why my
fingers won't stop bleeding

~~So take care how you sit and don't be greedy~~
~~be curious~~

he told me that I showed a great potential
that given how I turned his page's fame would
be a piece of coke but practice was essential
so like a virgin princess I believed ~~it~~ him
and golly who would ever have ~~behcieved~~ it
~~it's been ten years now and here now~~
~~I st full of my fear now and have~~
~~thirteen songs of it it but~~
I gave up school and mozart I vow to
make a new   rt and devote my time
to composing songs ~~like Whitney Houstons~~
now there ~~there~~ open back your eyes
be about trash because it's funny your
       fright

Lonesome Organist Rapes Page Turner

He told me that I knew just what to laugh at, and I want-ed to but — just could-n't ask — if he would take it back so I could know for cer - tain. — So on the bench I watched his left hand cros-sing, while dou-bl - ing en

that giv-en I turned heads and pag-es, fame would be a piece of cake, but prac-tice

was es-sen-tial. _____ So like a stu-pid chi-ld, I be-lieved it, ___

and gol-ly, who would ev-er had a-greed if ___ your gift for keep-ing truth and

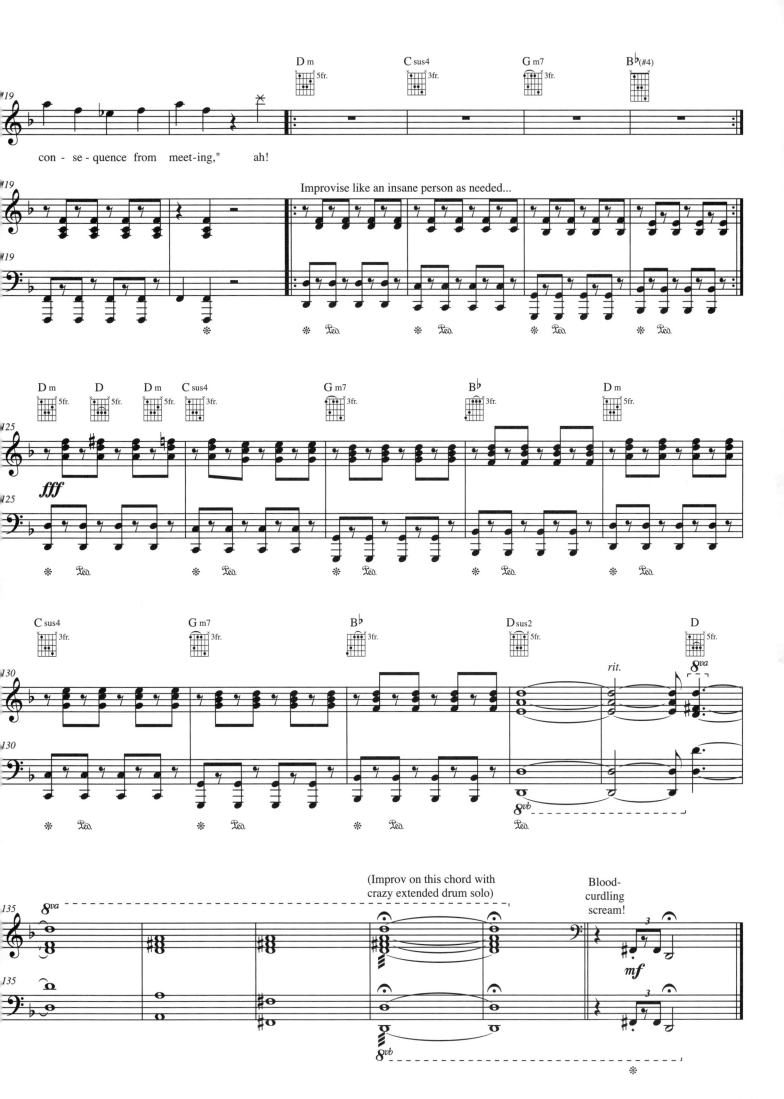

con - se - quence from meet-ing," ah!

Improvise like an insane person as needed...

(Improv on this chord with crazy extended drum solo)

Blood-curdling scream!

343

SORRY BUNCH

ah - we're a sorry bunch
no jury's out to lunch on this one darling
ah - we're a sorry ~~lot~~
~~the~~ ~~get~~
~~the~~ such an ~~anything~~ ~~~~
This is what we've got   So this got stalling

I could have lost ~~my~~ ~~~~ hand
you should look where you are going, ~~clumsy~~ guy
I could have lost ~~~~ ~~~~ ~~~~ my ~~~~ life
but I would lose ~~the~~ a hundred times
ah nah   just as long as you are

ah, we're a sorry bunch
no jury's out to lunch on this one

                    the
I could have lost ~~my~~ ~~~~way
than how the hell ~~could~~ we ~~~~ show up
I could have crissed ~~them~~ out
but I would skip a hundred parties

Sorry Bunch

346

The
KILL

The Kill

(b) I can't tell it like it is
~~the audience would listen~~
~~and they~~ nobody would listen
and now I've lost my train of thought
I tried too hard to find the words
to make you hear it's all so clear
here in my head it all makes sense

~~I am the~~
[I can't tell it like it is
the ~~point~~ story would ~~just~~ be missed]

a house or

~~think~~ what you will · I am the kill
the thing ~~that keeps~~ between the fire and meal

DM I have a tendency to exaggerate just a little bit
they're always telling me get the story straight or keep your mouth shut
there are no tragedies and no miracles unless you make them
it was true without the crap you added
why do you have to be so dramatic?

I am eleven feet, ok eight, ~~six~~ 6 feet three?
I am an architect? an architect? an art collector?
I am a architect? a ~~secretary? architect~~
~~etype~~ a rocket ship! a jet fighter! a paper airplane.
I have an ~~a~~ ~~xxxx~~
I fought the ~~xxxx~~ british and I won!

and I can't....

The Kill

The SHEEP SONG

red brush
washing up
painting north america
hush hush
don't don't rush
~~we~~ kills those who hurry up
~~[crossed out]~~

brown ~~[crossed out]~~ ~~[crossed out]~~ wine
turpentine ~~some things must not be~~ combined
~~all the pretty mixed~~ [crossed out]

now   now
still ~~somehow~~ anyhow
~~[crossed out]~~ we will make it ~~shake~~ somehow
~~maybe we can stuff it down~~

~~blue~~ ~~no simple way~~
~~given the [crossed out]~~   no simple ~~[crossed out]~~
maybe the ~~[crossed out]~~ i sink given ~~[crossed out]~~ you sink too
~~[crossed out]~~ won't know ~~[crossed out] looking~~ I think so

Gmaj/c min counting sheep I lay me down to sleep
but I see   a sheep that ~~you can't have~~ eat

shocked ~~through the door they're breaking in~~ in the nap
~~[crossed out] head~~ and my sheep is ~~[crossed out]~~ bed
they ~~[crossed out]~~   sent him off

The Sheep Song

in-vest in one with the si - lenc - er.   All of the stud-ies say if they're   calm when they die then they taste bet - ter.

calm when they die then they taste   bet - ter. _____   Ha   ha... _____

Ah   ha   ha...

BOSTON

Jason was Berlin
Glen was darlinghurst
seventh grade was Brad
we never got past first
you saw Julia last night
she just got in from L.A.
tomorrow you'll drive to the country
please say hi to all the family
have you heard the news from sydney
how'd you like to fly out with me
how'd you like to fly away from those machines
everywhere the spies are printing out our dreams
~~long lost~~ lovers ~~boozy~~ european parties sixty page ~~itineraries~~ itineraries
memories thick as bloody maries joseph jesus bloody hell
~~right~~ now we're here in boston
in love with downtown crossing   G/C/E/D/C
New York will still be there in the morning
come back ~~paris~~ to bed   my darling
~~Brookline~~ ~~Lexington~~ ~~the~~ in ∧ Spring
before we even met
Matt was pulling strings
and you were with Jeanette
hurry quick the phone is ringing is there someone you're expecting
there's a train at 7:30 we can catch it if we hurry
how'd you like to run away from these machines
hopes to working like you need no money
dancing like nobody's watching
loving like you've never had you're heart torn out
                                                    in ~~Burlington~~
tonight I'm yours in Boston   Lexington
right back where this all started
your face is somewhere ~~off~~ in scotland
come back to bed my darling
you can ~~write~~ put the details in a letter
The more embarrassing the better ~~no~~ talking
right now ~~it~~ ~~throw~~ is ~~no~~ ~~need~~ ~~for~~ ~~all~~ ~~the~~ ~~talking~~
right now ~~stuck~~ ~~to~~ ~~bed~~ I would just ~~like~~ to be in Boston...

Boston

366

375

9/06 – 1/13/07	Zero Arrow St.	Cambridge, MA	"The Onion Cellar" (40 performances)
-04-06	Roundhouse	London, UK	w/ The Red Paintings
-03-06	Roundhouse	London, UK	w/ The Red Paintings
-29-06	Starland Ballroom	Sayreville, NJ	w/ The Red Paintings
-28-06	Theatre of Living Arts	Philadelphia, PA	w/ The Red Paintings
-27-06	9:30 Club	Washington, D.C.	w/ The Red Paintings
-26-06	The Lincoln Theatre	Raleigh, NC	w/ The Red Paintings
-24-06	Variety Playhouse	Atlanta, GA	w/ The Red Paintings
-23-06	Bijou Theater	Knoxville, TN	w/ The Red Paintings
-21-06	Pageant	St. Louis, MO	w/ The Red Paintings
-20-06	Vic Theater	Chicago, IL	w/ The Red Paintings
-19-06	Pabst Theatre	Milwaukee, WI	w/ The Red Paintings
-18-06	First Avenue	Minneapolis, MN	w/ The Red Paintings
-15-06	Crystal Ballrom	Portland, OR	w/ The Red Paintings
-14-06	Showbox	Seattle, WA	w/ The Red Paintings
-13-06	Bimbos	San Francisco, CA	w/ The Red Paintings
-12-06	Bimbos	San Francisco, CA	w/ The Red Paintings
-10-06	Orpheum Theatre	Los Angeles, CA	w/ The Red Paintings
-09-06	SOMA	San Diego, CA	w/ The Red Paintings
-22-06	Heat	Perth, AUS	w/ The Red Paintings
-20-06	University Bar Level 5	Adelaide, Aus	w/ The Red Paintings
-18-06	The Corner Hotel	Melbourne, Aus	w/ The Red Paintings
-17-06	The Corner Hotel	Melbourne, Aus	w/ The Red Paintings
-16-06	The Roundhouse	Sydney, Aus	w/ The Red Paintings
-15-06	The Arena	Brisbane, Aus	w/ The Red Paintings
-13-06	Indigo	Wellington, NZ	w/ The Red Paintings
-12-06	King's Arms	Auckland, NZ	w/ The Red Paintings
-07-06	Shibuya Duo	Tokyo, Japan	
-03-06	Kesselhaus	Berlin, Germany	
-02-06	Kesselhaus	Hamburg, Germany	
-01-06	Zeche	Bochum, Germany	
-30-06	Backstage Werk	Munich, Germany	
-27-06	Reading Festival	Reading, UK	
-26-06	Monsters of Spex	Cologne, Germany	
-25-06	Leeds Festival	Leeds, UK	
-23-06	Spiegel Tent	Edinbugh, UK	
-19-06	Highfield Festival	Erfut, Germany	
-18-06	Pukkelpop Festival	Hasselt, Belgium	
-28-06	Croation Cultural Centre	Seattle, BC	w/ Panic! at the Disc, The Hush Sound
-27-06	Croation Cultural Centre	Vancouver, BC	w/ Panic! at the Disc, The Hush Sound
-26-06	Expo Center	Portland, OR	w/ Panic! at the Disc, The Hush Sound
-25-06	The Big Easy	Boise, ID	w/ Panic! at the Disc, The Hush Sound
-24-06	In The Venue	Salt Lake City, UT	w/ Panic! at the Disc, The Hush Sound
-22-06	The Fillmore	Denver, CO	w/ Panic! at the Disc, The Hush Sound
-21-06	The Uptown Theatre	Kansas City, MO	w/ Panic! at the Disc, The Hush Sound
-20-06	The Pageant	St. Louis, MO	w/ Panic! at the Disc, The Hush Sound
-19-06	Murat Egyptian Room	Indianapolis, IN	w/ Panic! at the Disc, The Hush Sound
-18-06	Chevrolet Amphitheatre	Pittsburgh, PA	w/ Panic! at the Disc, The Hush Sound
-16-06	Metropolis	Montreal, QUE	w/ Panic! at the Disc, The Hush Sound
-15-06	Molson Amphitheatre	Toronto, ON	w/ Panic! at the Disc, The Hush Sound
-14-06	State Theatre	Detroit, MI	w/ Panic! at the Disc, The Hush Sound
-13-06	Delta Plex	Grand Rapids, MI	w/ Panic! at the Disc, The Hush Sound
-12-06	Plain Dealer Pavilion	Cleveland, OH	w/ Panic! at the Disc, The Hush Sound
-11-06	Bogarts	Cincinnati, OH	w/ Panic! at the Disc, The Hush Sound
-09-06	Myth	St. Paul, MN	w/ Panic! at the Disc, The Hush Sound
-08-06	Summerfest	Millwaukee, WI	
-07-06	House of Blues	Chicago, IL	w/ Panic! at the Disc, The Hush Sound
-06-06	LC Pavilion	Columbus, OH	w/ Panic! at the Disc, The Hush Sound
-05-06	Dome Theater	Niagara Falls, NY	w/ Panic! at the Disc, The Hush Sound

07-04-06	Hampton Beach Casino Ballroom Hampton Beach, NH w/ Panic! at the Disco, The Hush Sound		
07-02-06	Discovery Meadow	San Jose, CA	w/ Violent Femmes, Lovemakers
07-01-06	Penns Landing	Philadelphia, PA	w/ Panic! at the Disc, The Hush Sound
06-30-06	Starland Ballroom	Sayerville, NJ	w/ Panic! at the Disc, The Hush Sound
06-29-06	Nokia Theater	New York, NY	w/ Panic! at the Disc, The Hush Sound
06-28-06	Nokia Theater	New York, NY	w/ Panic! at the Disc, The Hush Sound
06-27-06	9:30 Club	Washington, DC	w/ Panic! at the Disc, The Hush Sound
06-17-06	Bonnaroo	Manchester, TN	
06-04-06	Rock Im Park Festival	Nurnberg, GER	
06-03-06	Pinkpop Festival	Landgraaf, NL	
06-02-06	Rock Am Ring Festival	Nurburgring, GER	
05-31-06	Arena	Vienna, AUT	w/ Thomas Truax
05-30-06	Poshof	Linz, AUT	w/ Thomas Truax
05-28-06	ABART	Zurich, CH	w/ Thomas Truax
05-27-06	Fri-Son	Fribourg, CH	w/ Thomas Truax
05-26-06	Ninkasi	Lyon, FR	w/ Sires Band
05-25-06	Le Music Cafe	Mont De Marsan, FR	w/ Sires Band
05-23-06	Casa Das Artes	Famalicao, POR	w/ Thomas Truax
05-22-06	Moby Dick	Madrid, ESP	w/ Thomas Truax
05-20-06	Apolo	Barcelona, ESP	w/ Thomas Truax
05-19-06	La Ramier	Toulouse, FR	w/ DeVotchKa
05-18-06	Bataclan	Paris, FR	w/ DeVotchKa, Sires Band
05-17-06	Le Grand Mix	Tourcouing, FR	w/ DeVotchKa
05-16-06	Spiegel Tent	Hamburg, GER	w/ Serena Maneesch
05-14-06	Spiegel Tent	Berlin, GER	
05-13-06	AB	Brussells, BEL	w/ DeVotchKa, Thomas Truax
05-12-06	Astoria	London, UK	w/ DeVotchKa, Thomas Truax
05-11-06	Concorde 2	Brighton, UK	w/ DeVotchKa
05-10-06	Junction	Cambridge, UK	w/ DeVotchKa, Conscious Pilot
05-09-06	Academy	Birmingham, UK	w/ DeVotchKa
05-07-06	Leadmill	Sheffield, UK	w/ DeVotchKa
05-06-06	Academy 2	Manchester, UK	w/ DeVotchKa
05-05-06	Cat House	Glasgow, SCT	w/ DeVotchKa, William Douglas & The Wheel
05-04-06	Exchange	Edinburgh, SCT	w/ DeVotchKa, William Douglas & The Wheel
05-02-06	Temple Bar	Dublin, IRL	w/ Chuzzle
05-01-06	Limelight	Belfast, IRL	w/ Chuzzle, William Douglas & The Wheel
04-30-06	Danube Festival	Vienna, AUT	
04-29-06	Abaton	Prague, CZK	w/ Thomas Truax
04-27-06	Le Phenix	Bourges, FR	w/ Indochine
04-22-06	Webster Hall	New York, NY	w/ HUMANWINE
04-21-06	Orpheum	Boston, MA	w/ HUMANWINE, Porsches on the Autobahn
04-19-06	Jimmy Kimmel Live!	Los Angeles, CA	
04-18-06	Epicentre	San Diego, CA,	w/ David J, Reverend Glasseye
04-17-06	Clubhouse	Tempe, AZ	w/ Reverend Glasseye
04-09-06	Egg Theatre	Albany, NY	w/ Reverend Glasseye
04-08-06	Promowest Pavilion	Columbus, OH	w/ Ok Go!, Nine Black Alps
04-07-06	Metro	Chicago, IL	w/ Reverend Glasseye
04-05-06	Madrid Theatre	Kansas City, MO	w/ The Zeros
04-04-06	Bluebird Theater	Denver, CO	w/ Uphollow
04-03-06	In the Venue	Salt Lake City, UT	w/ Uphollow
03-16-06	Stubbs BBQ - SXSW	Austin, TX	w/ Gomez, Firey Furnaces
03-02-06	Ioka Theatre	Exeter, NH	w/ Reverend Glasseye
03-01-06	Biden Center @ Johnson State College	Johnson, VT	w/ Reverend Glasseye
02-04-06	Museum of Fine Arts	Boston, MA	Amanda Palmer Solo w/ Jaggery & Jason Web
02-03-06	Joe's Pub	New York, NY	Amanda Palmer Solo
12-31-05	Concourse Exhibition Center San Francisco, CA w/ The String Cheese Incident, Yard Dog Road Show, Vau De Vire Society, Lorin (Bassnectar), El Circo		
12-30-05	Concourse Exhibition Center San Francisco, CA w/ The String Cheese Incident, Yard Dog Road Show, Vau De Vire Society, Lorin (Bassnectar), El Circo		
12-29-05	Henry Fonda Theatre	Los Angeles, CA	w/ Janet Klein and Her Parlor Boys
12-28-05	RecCenter Space	Los Angeles, CA	

0-31-05	Avalon	Boston, MA	w/ Devotchka & Faun Fables
0-29-05	Lupos	Providence, RI	w/ Devotchka & Faun Fables
0-28-05	Webster Hall	New York, NY	w/ Devotchka & Faun Fables
0-27-05	Higher Ground	Burlington, VT	w/ Devotchka & Faun Fables
0-26-05	Club Soda	Montreal, QUE	w/ Devotchka & Faun Fables
0-25-05	Mod Club	Toronto, ON	w/ Devotchka & Faun Fables
0-23-05	Town Hall	Buffalo, NY	w/ Devotchka & Faun Fables
0-22-05	Mr. Small's Theater	Pittsburgh, PA	w/ Devotchka & Faun Fables
0-21-05	Newport Music Hall	Columbus, OH	w/ Devotchka & Faun Fables
0-20-05	St. Andrews Hall	Detroit, MI	w/ Devotchka & Faun Fables
0-18-05	The Intersection	Grand Rapids, MI	w/ Devotchka & Faun Fables
0-17-05	Barrymore Theatre	Madison, WI	w/ Devotchka & Faun Fables
0-15-05	Metro	Chicago, IL	w/ Devotchka & Faun Fables
0-14-05	Englert Theatre	Iowa City, IA	w/ Devotchka & Faun Fables
0-13-05	Madrid Theatre	Kansas City, MO	w/ Devotchka & Faun Fables
0-12-05	Fox Theatre	Boulder, CO	w/ Devotchka & Faun Fables
0-06-05	Christopher Lydon Radio Show	Boston, MA	
8-25-05	ABC	Glasgow, SCT	Amanda Palmer SOLO
8-24-05	Fringe Festival	Edinburgh, SCT	Amanda Palmer SOLO
8-22-05	Moshulu	Aberdeen, SCT	Amanda Palmer SOLO
7-30-05	Fuji Rock Festival	Niigata, JAP	
7-20-05	Paradise Lounge	Boston, MA	Amanda Palmer SOLO
7-02-05	Roskilde Festival	Roskilde, DEN	
7-01-05	Rock Werchter Festival	Werchter, BEL	
6-26-05	Glastonbury Festival	Pilton, UK	
6-24-05	Wireless Festival	London, UK	w/ Moby, Psychedelic Furs
6-23-05	Royal Albert Hall	London, UK	
6-22-05	Zenith	Paris, FR	w/ Nine Inch Nails
6-21-05	Nouveau Casino	Paris, FR	
6-19-05	Sherwood Festival	Padova, IT	
6-18-05	The Velvet Club	Rimini, IT	
6-15-05	Columbiahalle	Berlin, Ger	w/ Nine Inch Nails
6-14-05	The Arena	Vienna, Aus	w/ Nine Inch Nails
6-12-05	Download Festival	Derby, UK	
6-11-05	Hurricane Festival	Neuhausen, GER	
6-10-05	Southside Festival	Scheessel, GER	
6-07-05	Avalon	Boston, MA	
6-05-05	Paradise	Boston, MA	
6-02-05	Sports Palace	Mexico City, MEX	w/ Nine Inch Nails
5-31-05	Soma	San Diego, CA	w/ Nine Inch Nails
5-30-05	Soma	San Diego, CA	w/ Nine Inch Nails
5-29-05	Marquee Theater	Phoenix, AZ	w/ Trail of Dead
5-28-05	Marquee Theater	Phoenix, AZ	w/ Nine Inch Nails
5-27-05	Marquee Theater	Phoenix, AZ	w/ Nine Inch Nails
5-25-05	Stubb's BBQ	Austin, TX	w/ Nine Inch Nails
5-24-05	Verison WirelessTheater	Houston, TX	w/ Nine Inch Nails
5-22-05	Tabernacle	Atlanta, GA	w/ Nine Inch Nails
5-21-05	Tabernacle	Atlanta, GA	w/ Nine Inch Nails
5-20-05	9:30 Club	Washington, DC	
5-19-05	The Electric Factory	Philadelphia, PA	w/ Nine Inch Nails
5-18-05	The Electric Factory	Philadelphia, PA	w/ Nine Inch Nails
5-16-05	The Hammerstein Ballroom	New York, NY	w/ Nine Inch Nails
5-15-05	The Hammerstein Ballroom	New York, NY	w/ Nine Inch Nails
5-14-05	Northern Lights	Clifton Park, NY	
5-13-05	Orpheum Theater	Boston, MA	w/ Nine Inch Nails
5-12-05	Orpheum Theater	Boston, MA	w/ Nine Inch Nails
5-10-05	Koolhaus	Toronto, ONT	w/ Nine Inch Nails
5-09-05	Koolhaus	Toronto, ONT	w/ Nine Inch Nails
5-07-05	The Congress Theatre	Chicago, IL	w/ Nine Inch Nails
5-06-05	The Congress Theatre	Chicago, IL	w/ Nine Inch Nails
5-06-05	Mancow Radio Show	Chicago, IL	

Date	Venue	Location	Support
05-05-05	The Pageant	St. Louis, MO	
05-04-05	The Fillmore	Denver, CO	w/ Nine Inch Nails
05-03-05	The Fillmore	Denver, CO	w/ Nine Inch Nails
05-01-05	Coachella Festival	Indio, CA	
04-29-05	The Joint	Las Vegas	w/ Nine Inch Nails
04-29-05	Empire	Sacramento, CA	w/ Menomena
04-28-05	The Warfield	San Francisco, CA	w/ Nine Inch Nails
04-27-05	The Warfield	San Francisco, CA	w/ Nine Inch Nails
04-26-05	Great American Music Hall	San Francisco, CA	w/ Vau de Vire Society, Rosin Coven
04-24-05	Paradise	Boston, MA	w/ Fluttr Effect, Thomas Truax
04-22-05	Club Liquid	Manchester, NH	w/ Bon Savants
04-10-05	House of Blues	Cleveland, OH	w/ Buck 65
04-09-05	Promowest Pavilion	Columbus, OH	w/ ASH, The Black Keys, The Bravery
04-09-05	CD 101 In-Studio	Columbus, OH	
04-08-05	American University	Washington, DC	
04-07-05	The Norva	Norfolk, VA	
04-06-05	The Stone Pony	Asbury Park, NJ	
03-31-05	The Astoria	London, UK	w/ Nine Inch Nails
03-30-05	The Astoria	London, UK	w/ Nine Inch Nails
03-17-05	Club LR	Toulouse, FR	
03-16-05	Mars Attack	Angouleme, FR	
03-15-05	Le Rock School Barbey	Bordeaux, FR	
03-13-05	Le Grand Mix	Tourcoing, FR	
03-12-05	Le Noumatrouff	Mulhouse, FR	
03-11-05	L'Espace	Sannois, FR	w/ Teen Machine
03-10-05	Transbordeur	Lyon, FR	
03-08-05	Gaswerk	Winterthur, CH	w/ Roman Revutsky
03-07-05	Atomic Cafe	Munich, GER	w/ M.A.S.S.
03-06-05	Mousonturm	Frankfurt, GER	w/ M.A.S.S.
03-05-05	Gebaude	Cologne, GER	w/ The Surreal Funfair
03-03-05	Star Club	Dresden, GER	w/ M.A.S.S.
03-02-05	Logo	Hamburg, GER	w/ M.A.S.S.
02-28-05	Abaton	Prague, CZ	
02-27-05	Flex	Vienna, AT	
02-26-05	Transylvania	Milan, ITA	
02-25-05	New Age Club	Treviso, ITA	w/ The Flash Express
02-23-05	La Boule Noire	Paris, FR	w/ Teen Machine
02-22-05	Handelsbeurs	Gent, BEL	
02-21-05	Melkweg	Amsterdam, HOL	
02-19-05	The Scala	London, UK	w/ Gisli
02-18-05	The Liverpool Academy	Liverpool, UK	w/ Gisli
02-17-05	The Venue	Edinburgh, SCT	w/ Gisli
02-06-05	The Space	Portland, ME	w/ Regina Spektor
02-06-05	Bullmoose Records In-Store Apperance	Portland, ME	
02-05-05	Lupos	Providence, RI	w/ Regina Spektor
02-04-05	Theater of the Living Arts	Philadelphia, PA	w/ Regina Spektor
02-03-05	Toads Place	New Haven, CT	w/ Regina Spektor
01-28-05	Zoes Nigthclub	San Jose, CA	w/ Collective Soul
01-27-05	Harlows	Sacramento, CA	w/ Groovie Ghoulies
01-26-05	Velvet Jones	Santa Barbara, CA	w/ Apex Theroy
01-25-05	The Sets	Tempe, AZ	w/ Razorlight, The Reflections
01-23-05	Music Cafe @ Plan B	Park City, UT	w/ Nellie MaKay
01-22-05	Music Cafe @ Plan B - late show	Park City, UT	
01-22-05	Music Cafe @ Plan B - early show	Park City, UT	w/, Saul Williams
01-01-05	Liberty Hall	Lawrence, KS	w/ Matson Jones
12-31-04	4th And B	San Diego, CA	w/ Blues Explosion
12-17-04	Ding Dong Lounge	Melbourne, AUS	w/ Love of Diagrams
12-16-04	Annadale Hotel	Sydney, AUS	w/ Bra Code and K.K. Chuggy
12-15-04	The Zoo	Brisbane, AUS	w/ Charles Foster Kane
12-13-04	Kings Arms	Auckland, NZ	w/ Faun Fables and Fats White
12-09-04	Medicine Bar	Birmingham, UK	

Date	Venue	City	With
?-08-04	Life Cafe	Manchester, UK	
?-07-04	Cargo	London, UK	
?-04-04	Brreekmolen / Petrol	Antwerp, BEL	
?-03-04	Paard Van Troje	Den Haag, NL	
?-02-04	Salle La Pleide	Tours, FR	w/ Katzenjammer Kabaret
?-01-04	La Laitere	Strasbourg, FR	w/ Katzenjammer Kabaret
-30-04	Pop & Glow @ English Theater-Frankfurt, GER		
-29-04	Kalkscheune	Berlin, GER	
-20-04	Epicentre	San Diego, CA	w/ Count Zero, Ditty Bops
-19-04	El Rey Theater	Los Angeles, CA	w/ Count Zero, Ditty Bops
-17-04	Great American Music Hall	San Francisco, CA	w/ Count Zero, Ditty Bops
-15-04	Aladdin Theater	Portland, OR	w/ Count Zero, Ditty Bops
-13-04	Red Room	Vancouver , BC	w/ Count Zero, Ditty Bops
-12-04	Neumos	Seattle , WA	w/ Count Zero, Ditty Bops
-09-04	In the Venue	Salt Lake City , UT	w/ Count Zero, Ditty Bops
-08-04	Bluebird Theater	Denver, CO	w/ Count Zero, Ditty Bops
-06-04	Mississippi Nights	St. Louis, MO	w/ Count Zero, Ditty Bops
-05-04	Park West	Chicago, IL	w/ Count Zero, Ditty Bops
-03-04	Mod Club Theater	Toronto, ONT	w/ Count Zero, Ditty Bops
-02-04	Cabaret Music Hall	Montreal, QUE	w/ Count Zero, Ditty Bops
?-31-04	Pearl Street	Northampton, MA	w/ Count Zero, Ditty Bops
?-30-04	Avalon	Boston, MA	w/ Count Zero, Tiger Lilies
?-29-04	Bowery Ballroom	New York, NY	w/ Count Zero, Ditty Bops
?-27-04	Black Cat	Washington, DC	w/ Count Zero
?-24-04	Orange Peel	Asheville , NC	w/ Count Zero
?-23-04	Headliners	Columbia , SC	w/ Count Zero
?-22-04	Cats Cradle	Carborro , NC	
?-20-04	Club Downunder	Tallahassee , FL	w/ Count Zero
?-19-04	State Theater	St. Petersberg , FL	w/ Count Zero
?-17-04	Uptown Theater	Kansas City, MO	w/ Sonic Youth, The Music
?-16-04	CRIMINAL RECORDS	Atlanta, GA	
?-16-04	Echo Lounge	Atlanta, GA	w/ Count Zero
?-15-04	40 Watt Club	Athens, GA	w/ Count Zero, Gogol Bordello
?-13-04	Workplay Theater	Birmingham, AL	w/ Count Zero
?-12-04	One Eyed Jacks	New Orleans, LA	w/ Count Zero, Baby Rosebud
?-10-04	Gypsy Tea Room	Dallas, TX	w/ Count Zero
?-09-04	Walters on Washington	Houston, TX	w/ Count Zero
?-08-04	EMO's	Austin, TX	w/ Count Zero
?-02-04	Debaser Club	Stockholm, SWE	w/ Yumi Yumi
30-04	Barend en van Dorp	Hilversum, HOL	
29-04	AB Club	Brussels, BEL	
29-04	La Boule Noire	Paris, FRA	w/ Katzenjammer Kabaret
27-04	Atomic Cafe	Munich, GER	
26-04	Prime Club	Cologne, GER	
24-04	Knaack Klub	Berlin, GER	
22-04	Molotow	Hamburg, GER	w/ Fast Forward & Spex
21-04	Melkweg	Amsterdam, NET	w/ Juliet's Ghost
20-04	Madame JoJo's	London, UK	
11-04	Bennington College	Bennington, VT	
10-04	Living Room	Providence, RI	
22-04	Crocodile Café	Seattle, WA	
21-04	Dantes	Portland, OR	
20-04	Café Du Nord	San Francisco, CA	w/ Charming Hostess
19-04	Jimmy Kimmel Live	Hollywood, CA	
18-04	Troubador	Los Angeles, CA	w/ The Centimeters
17-04	The Casbah	San Diego, CA	w/ Bunky
15-04	7th St. Entry	Minneapolis, MN	w/ Devotchka
14-04	Schubas	Chicago, IL	w/ Devotchka
13-04	Magic Stick	Detroit, MI	w/ Devotchka
12-04	El Mocambo	Toronto, ON	w/ The Lost Cause
11-04	The Main Room	Montreal, QC	w/ Shoot the Moon
7-04	Haldren Pop Festival	Dusseldorf, GER	w/ Keane

7-09-04	Paradise	Boston, MA	w/ Rev. Glass Eye & His Wooden Legs
6-29-04	Le Reservoir	Paris, FRA	
6-24-04	The Viper Room	Los Angeles, CA	w/ Julia Fly
6-19-04	Beachcomber	Wellfleet, MA	
6-18-04	The Space	Portland, ME	w/ Subject Bias
6-17-04	Maxwell's	Hoboken, NJ	w/ The Mint Chicks
6-1-04	Middle East	Boston, MA	w/ Legendary Pink Dots
5-14-04	Theater of Living Arts	Philadelphia, PA	w/ Mission of Burma
5-22-04	Avalon	Boston, MA	w/ Mission of Burma
4-28-04	Tribeca Rock Club	New York, NY	w/ Mindless Self Indulgence
4-24-04	The Middle East	Cambridge, MA	
4-10-04	Rudy's	New Haven, CT	.
4-9-04	The Milky Way	Jamaica Plain, MA	
4-8-04	Lexington High School	Lexington, MA	w/ Quay
4-1-04	The Black Cat	Washington, DC	w/ Two if by Sea
3-30-04	The Cave	Chapel Hill, NC	
3-29-04	Geno's Sports Bar	Boone, NC	w/ The Dandy Lions
3-27-04	The Echo Lounge	Atlanta, GA	w/ Ester Drang
3-26-04	The Caravan	Memphis, TN	w/ Oliver's Army, Both Hands Broken
3-25-04	Big Boys Q'n	Carbondale, IL	w/ Eyecandy
3-23-04	Frederick's Music Lounge	St. Louis, MO	w/ Danny Black
3-22-04	The Music Cafe	Columbia, MO	w/ Demolition Doll Rods
3-17-04	The Hard Rock Cafe	Austin, TX	SXSW Showcase
3-14-04	Pabst Theater	Milwaukee, WI	w/ Sleepytime Gorilla Museum and Faun Fables
3-13-04	The Bottom Lounge	Chicago, IL	
3-12-04	Radio Radio	Indianapolis, IN	w/ Sleepytime Gorilla Museum and Faun Fables
3-11-04	Grog Shop	Cleveland Heights, OH	w/ Sleepytime Gorilla Museum and Faun Fable
3-10-04	Northstar Bar	Philadelphia, PA	w/ Sleepytime Gorilla Museum and Faun Fables
3-9-04	Axis	Boston, MA	w/ Sleepytime Gorilla Museum and Faun Fables
3-6-04	The Space	Hamden, CT	w/ Ladyfriend, AwRy
3-5-04	The Living Room	Providence, RI	.
3-2-04	Tonic	New York, NY	w/ Sleepytime Gorilla Museum and Barbez
3-1-04	Tonic	New York, NY	w/ Sleepytime Gorilla Museum and Faun Fables
2-27-04	The Larimer Lounge	Denver, CO	w/ J Mascis
2-24-04	The Bug Jar	Rochester, NY	w/ Thought, Joanna McNaney
2-23-04	Valentine's	Albany, NY	w/ Sun Also Rising
2-22-04	DIY Shows	New Brunswick, NJ	w/ Burn The Mountain Down
2-21-04	Bard College	Annandale-on-Hudson, NY	.
2-16-04	Iota	Arlington, VA	w/ Cigarbox Planetarium
2-15-04	Club Laga	Pittsburgh, PA	w/ Bella Morte
2-14-04	The Sanctuary	Stroudsburg, PA	
2-13-04	Doc Watson's	Philadelphia, PA	
2-10-04	Joe's Pub	New York, NY	.
2-6-04	Wesleyan University	Middletown, CT	
2-3-04	Iron Horse Music Hall	Northampton, MA	
1-30-04	Curly's Coffee	Amherst, NH	
1-25-04	The Middle East	Cambridge, MA	w/ World/Inferno Friendship Society, SNMNMNM and Lycaon Pictus
1-24-04	The Lucky Dog	Worcester, MA	
1-17-04	The Flywheel	Easthampton, MA	w/ The Chemical Wedding, Captain Shy
1-16-04	Arisia	Boston, MA	w/ Molly Zenobia
1-13-04	The Zeitgeist Gallery	Cambridge, MA	
1-10-04	The Green Room	Providence, RI	w/ Eryss, The Eyesores, Seratonin
1-8-04	Bullmoose Music	Portsmouth, NH	In-store performance
1-8-04	The Space	Portland, ME